Reason and the Heart

A volume in the series

Cornell Studies in the Philosophy of Religion

EDITED BY WILLIAM P. ALSTON

A full list of titles in the series appears at the end of the book.

William J. Wainwright

Reason and the Heart

*A Prolegomenon to a Critique
of Passional Reason*

Cornell University Press, Ithaca and London

First published 1995 by Cornell University Press.

Printed in the United States of America

⊗ The paper in this book meets the minimum requirements
of the American National Standard for Information Sciences—
Permanence of Paper for Printed Library Materials, ANSI Z39.48-1984.

Library of Congress Cataloging-in-Publication Data

Wainwright, William J.
Reason and the heart : a prolegomenon to a critique of passional reason /
William J. Wainwright
p.   cm.—(Cornell studies in the philosophy of religion)
Includes bibliographical references and index.
ISBN 0–8014–3139–5 (alk. paper)
1. Faith and reason.   2. Faith and reason—Christianity.   3. Subjectivity—
Religious aspects.   4. Subjectivity—Religious aspects—Christianity.
5. Edwards, Jonathan, 1708–1758. 6. Newman, John Henry, 1801–1890.
7. James, William, 1842–1910. I. Title. II. Series.
BL51.W16   1995
210—dc20   95–18022

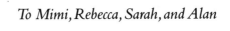
To Mimi, Rebecca, Sarah, and Alan

Contents

Acknowledgments

The second section of Chapter 1 first appeared as "Jonathan Edwards and the Sense of the Heart" (*Faith and Philosophy* 7 [January 1990], 43–62). The third and fourth sections of Chapter 1 and the first section of Chapter 4 are drawn from "The Nature of Reason: Locke, Swinburne, and Edwards" (in *Reason and the Christian Religion*, ed. Alan Padgett [Oxford: Oxford University Press, 1994]). Chapter 3 is a revised version of "James, Rationality, and Religious Belief" (*Religious Studies* 27 [June 1991], 223–38, © Cambridge University Press 1991. Reprinted with the permission of Cambridge University Press). A shorter version of the second section of Chapter 4 appeared as section 5 of "World-Views, Criteria, and Epistemic Circularity" (in *Inter-Religious Models and Criteria*, ed. James Kellenberger [London: Macmillan; New York: St. Martin's Press, 1993]). Chapter 5 is a descendant of "Does Disagreement Imply Relativism?" (*International Philosophical Quarterly* 26 [March 1986], 47–60). I thank the publishers and editors involved for permission to reuse this material. I also thank Richard Gale and William Rowe for permission to quote from correspondence. Work on Chapter 1 was supported by a summer grant from the National Endowment for the Humanities. Chapter 2 was completed with the help of a summer research grant from the Graduate School of the University of Wisconsin–Milwaukee. Chapter 3 was written during my tenure as a

Fellow at the University's Center for Twentieth-Century Studies. I am very grateful for this support. I would finally like to thank our departmental secretaries, Saqunda Pica and Mary DeBuhr, who typed the final versions of the manuscript. I am grateful also to Brenda Williams, who typed what must have seemed endless early drafts of the book and who died unexpectedly in the late winter of 1993.

W. J. W.

Reason and the Heart

Introduction:
Evidence and the Heart

In *An Essay concerning Human Understanding*, John Locke defines reason as "the discovery of the certainty or probability of such propositions or truths, which the mind arrives at by deduction made from such ideas, which it has got by the use of its natural faculties; viz. by sensation or reflection" (4.18.2). Rational belief is proportionate to the strength of the evidence at one's disposal. "The mind, if it *will proceed rationally*, ought to examine all the grounds of probability, and see how they make more or less for or against any proposition, before it assents to or dissents from it; and upon a due balancing of the whole, reject or receive it, with more or less firm assent, proportionably to the preponderancy of the greater grounds of probability on one side or the other" (4.15.5). What is true of beliefs in general is true of religious beliefs. They are rational only if they are (1) properly basic (by being immediately grounded, for example, in the mind's intuitive awareness of its own ideas), or (2) inferred from those ideas by sound deductive or inductive standards, or (3) the content of a revelation whose credentials are certified by beliefs meeting the first or second condition. Although modern intellectuals may doubt whether religious beliefs meet these standards, Locke did not. God's existence can be demonstrated, and the evidence at our disposal makes it probable that the Bible is God's revelation.

Locke's view is sometimes called evidentialism. Religious beliefs are rationally held if and only if one has sufficient evidence for them.[1] Although evidentialism is currently unfashionable,[2] it has much to be said for it. Religious beliefs, like scientific beliefs, *appear* to be "evidence-essential"—they are rationally held only if one has reason to believe that someone in one's intellectual community has good evidence for them. (I am entitled to believe there are quarks, for example, but only because I have reason to believe that physicists have evidence for them.)[3] Religious beliefs are also controversial. Responsible inquirers have called them into question, and some doubts about them are not unreasonable. Under these conditions one can appropriately be asked what entitles one to believe. The only entitlement that is likely to convince others of one's right to believe is good evidence. But finally (and most important), Christians have often assumed that there *is* good evidence for their position and that those who examine it without prejudice will be persuaded by it.

These considerations do not entail that a person does not have an epistemic right to believe unless she can provide good evidence for her belief. But they do imply that she must believe that there *is* good evidence for them, and that some people (the community's theologians or saints perhaps) have it. At the very least, they suggest that evidentially based religious beliefs play a more important role in the life of mature Christians than many contemporary philosophers of religion are prepared to admit.[4]

1. As it stands this claim is ambiguous. A belief is *subjectively* rational on this view if and only if one has what one *believes* to be good evidence for it and, in holding one's belief, has not violated any epistemic duties. One's belief is *objectively* rational if and only if it is subjectively rational, and one's evidence is *in fact* good evidence for it. I will ignore this ambiguity in what follows since it is not important for my purposes.

2. Its two most significant opponents are Alvin Plantinga and Nicholas Wolterstorff, but their attacks on evidentialism have won widespread support. Some prominent theistic philosophers, however, *are* evidentialists. Richard Swinburne is an example.

3. I owe this point to Stephen J. Wykstra. See his "Toward a Sensible Evidentialism: On the Notion of 'Needing Evidence,'" in *Philosophy of Religion: Selected Readings*, ed. William L. Rowe and William J. Wainwright (Orlando, Fla.: Harcourt, Brace, Jovanovich, 1989).

4. Plantinga has argued that although mature theists may *have* good evidence for their beliefs and know that they have it, their beliefs are not *based* on their evidence.

Two interrelated facts have contributed to the current tendency to downplay the importance of evidence in the formation and retention of religious beliefs. The first is the obvious absence of evidence that would compel the assent of any fully informed, sufficiently intelligent, and adequately trained inquirer. The second is the fact that religious belief seems to depend more directly on the state of one's heart or moral temperament than on evidence. How else explain why two equally intelligent and informed inquirers can arrive at such different assessments of the same evidence. (Compare Richard Swinburne's and J. L. Mackie's evaluations of the evidence for design, for example.)

This book provides a different account of these facts. We will examine the thesis that mature religious belief can, and perhaps should, be based on evidence but that the evidence can be accurately assessed only by men and women who possess the proper moral and spiritual qualifications.

This view was once a Christian commonplace; reason is capable of knowing God on the basis of evidence—but only when one's cognitive faculties are rightly disposed. It should be distinguished from two other views that have dominated modern thought. The first claims that God can be known by "objective reason," that is, by an understanding that systematically excludes passion, desire, and emotion from the process of reasoning. The other insists that God can be known only "subjectively," or by the heart. Both views identify reason with ratiocination. They also assume that reasoning is objective only when unaffected by wants, interests, and desires. The tradition I will discuss steers between these two extremes. It places a high value on proofs, arguments, and inferences yet also believes that a properly disposed heart is needed to see their *force*.

This may be true in some cases. I think, however, that if evidence is construed sufficiently broadly (so as to include nonpropositional as well as propositional evidence, for example), and if the "based on" relation is not restricted to self-conscious inference, Plantinga's proposition is not true in most cases. I think, in other words, that if they came to believe that *all* the evidence at their disposal was worthless even mature Christians would, for the most part, find it impossible to retain their beliefs. It should be noted that this broad understanding of evidence and the "based on" relation is common among evidentialists.

This epistemic theory is deeply embedded in important strands of the Christian tradition. Calvin, for example, thought that rational arguments for the authority of scripture "will not obtain full credit in the hearts of men until they are sealed by the inward testimony of the Spirit."[5] And even though Aquinas believed that there is good evidence for the divine origin of Christian teaching, he did not think that it was sufficient to compel assent without the inward movement of a will grounded in a "supernatural principle."[6] Similarly, seventeenth-century Anglican divines argued that "the gospel can only obtain, 'a free admission into the assent of the understanding, when it brings a passport from a rightly disposed will.' "[7] The notion that a proper disposition is needed to appreciate the force of rational arguments for the authority of the gospel can easily be extended to rational arguments for the truths of "natural religion" when these, too, come under attack. John Spurr has argued that this process was well under way by the end of the seventeenth century.[8]

One of the most carefully elaborated articulations of this position is that of Jonathan Edwards. In Chapter 1, I discuss his position in detail. The chapter is divided into four sections. The first describes his ambiguous attitudes toward reason. The second section discusses the epistemic consequences of the new heart received by the converted. The third section shows why Edwards thought that moral and spiritual qualifications are needed to appreciate the force of evidence for religious truths. The fourth section discusses Edwards's relation to evidentialism. Throughout the chapter I shall be implicitly arguing that Edwards's epistemological position is plausible provided that his theistic metaphysics is sound.

Chapters 2 and 3 examine John Henry Newman and William James. I shall argue that their positions are similar in important re-

5. Calvin, *Institutes of the Christian Religion* (Grand Rapids, Mich.: Eerdmans, 1957) vol. 1, book 1, chap. 7, sec. 4.
6. Saint Thomas Aquinas, *The Summa Theologica* (New York: Benziger, 1947), vol. 2, part II–II, quest. 6, art. 1.
7. John Spurr, " 'Rational Religion' in Restoration England," *Journal of the History of Ideas* 49 (1988), 580. The internal quote is from Robert South (*Sermons* [5 vols.; Oxford: 1842], vol. 1, 116).
8. Ibid.

spects to Edwards's. But each has something of his own to add. Newman's most important contribution is his demonstration that the
properties Edwards finds in religious reasoning are features of *all* reasoning. Inquiry in the humanities and social sciences, in everyday
life, and even in science unavoidably reflects what William James
called our "willing" or "passional" nature—our temperament, needs,
concerns, fears, hopes, passions, and "divinations." But neither
Newman nor James thinks that the influence of our passional nature
should be deplored; its effects can be epistemically beneficial as well
as harmful. Newman's position, like Edwards's, depends on the truth
of theistic metaphysics. Part of the interest of William James's version
of these themes is that his does not depend on theistic metaphysics,
although it does rest on certain very general claims about the nature
of reality that could appropriately be called religious.

What all three have in common is the following: (1) Edwards and
Newman believe there is good evidence for religious truths. I shall
show that, contrary to standard interpretations, James does so as
well. (2) All three believe that proper epistemic functioning depends
on the possession of the appropriate moral or spiritual temperament.
A converted heart, or a sensitive conscience, or a demand for meaning and the possibility of significant action are needed to appreciate
the force of the evidence for religious truths. (3) Each believes that
(when properly disciplined) our passional nature tracks the truth.
"Passional reason" is reliable. Edwards and Newman base this contention on their theistic metaphysics. James's position is less overtly
theistic, but it too rests on general claims about the ultimate nature
of reality.

Chapter 4 discusses the two most important objections to this
view. The first is that it is epistemically and morally objectionable to
allow our beliefs to be influenced by our passional nature. Our
wishes and desires are unreliable guides to truth, and a person who
indulges them is to be pitied if not blamed. The second is the apparent circularity of these views. Edwards defends the claim that the
converted heart is correlated with the way things are by appealing to
a form of theistic metaphysics that is deeply embedded in a specific
theological tradition. Newman's defense of the epistemic propriety
of what he calls "illative reasoning" is similar. The circle in James is

less obvious because his arguments do not clearly rest on the truth of the metaphysical hypotheses (supernaturalism, indeterminism, meliorism, and so on) that he will erect on their basis. But would we find them persuasive if we were not already predisposed to think that reality is "friendly" to us and not "foreign"? The critical response to James suggests not.

Both objections can be met. The first begs the question, and the circle is not vicious since a similar circularity infects *all* informal reasoning.

Chapter 5 addresses the fear of relativism. I shall argue that although the view described in Chapters 1 through 3 implies that agreement among rational and informed inquirers is unlikely, it does not imply that either truth or our standards of rationality are only relatively valid.

The Epilogue explains why we should take views such as Edwards's seriously. It concludes by offering suggestions as to how one might construct a "critique of passional reason," an account of the conditions under which passion does and does not enhance reasoning.

I am inclined to believe that the thesis I will be discussing is essentially correct. The book's purpose will be accomplished, however, if it succeeds in placing a neglected view back on the table and convinces its readers that positions such as Edwards's are more difficult to refute than they previously may have thought.

1

Jonathan Edwards
and the Heart

Jonathan Edwards was strongly influenced by continental rationalists such as Malebranche, by some of the Cambridge Platonists (Henry More, for example), and by the empiricists (especially Locke). He was also excited by Newton and the new science. Although these traditions were diverse, they had an important feature in common—an almost uncritical confidence in reason's power and scope. Edwards's practice reflects this confidence. Philosophical arguments are deployed to demolish critics, justify the principal Christian doctrines, and erect a speculative metaphysics (a subjective idealism like Berkeley's). But Edwards was also a Calvinist who shared the Reformed tradition's distrust of humanity's natural capacities and its skepticism about natural theology.

The impact of these diverse strands is reflected in the apparent ambiguity of Edwards's remarks on reason. Thus, on the one hand, he can say that, "arguing for the being of a God according to the natural powers from everything we are conversant with is short, easy, and what we naturally fall into" (Misc. 268, T 78)[1] or claim that we can

---

1. Jonathan Edwards's principal discussions of reason are located in the "Miscellanies" (a number of which can be found in *The Philosophy of Jonathan Edwards from His Private Notebooks*, ed. Harvey G. Townsend [Eugene, Ore.: University of Oregon Monographs, 1955], hereafter Misc. T; "A Divine and Supernatural Light" and "Miscellaneous Observations" (in *The Works of President Edwards* [New York:

know that a just God governs the world by the "light of nature."
Conscience that sees "the relation and agreement there is between
that which is wrong or unjust and punishment" and finds unpun-
ished wrongs "shocking" naturally leads us to conclude that God is
"a just being" (Misc. 353, T 110–111). Yet he can also insist that, in
thinking about God, reason is baffled by "mystery," "paradox," and
"seeming inconsistence." (Examples are an omnipresence without
extension, an immutability [which Edwards thinks implies duration]
without succession, and the idea of a "perfect knowledge of all . . .
things of external sense, without any sensation or any reception of
ideas from without" [Misc. 1340, T 231].) Even though "the invisible things of God are indeed to be understood by the things that are
made," uninstructed reason invariably errs (Misc. 986, T 212). It is
"almost impossible [for example] for unassisted reason" to demonstrate "that the world, and all things contained therein, are effects,
and had a beginning." A person who was "left to himself" "would
be apt to reason" that because causes and effects must be "similar and
conformable, matter must have a material cause" and "evil and ir-
regularity . . . must be attributed to an evil and unwise cause." Indeed, without assistance, "the best reasoner in the world . . . might
be led into the grossest errors and contradictions" (Misc. Obs.,
185–86). If "God never speaks to or converses at all with mankind,"
we would most likely think "there is no being that made and governs

---

B. Franklin, 1968; reprint of the Leeds edition reissued with a two-volume supple-
ment in Edinburgh, 1847], vol. VIII), hereafter DSL and Misc. Obs., respectively;
"The Mind," "Subjects to Be Handled in the Treatise on the Mind," and "Of the
Prejudices of Imagination" (in *Scientific and Philosophical Writings*, ed. Wallace E. An-
derson [New Haven: Yale University Press, 1980], hereafter Mind, Subjects, and
Prejudices, respectively; and *Original Sin* (Boston 1758; reprint, New Haven: Yale
University Press, 1970), hereafter OS. Other relevant material can be found in *Religious Affections* (Boston 1746; reprint, New Haven: Yale University Press, 1959),
hereafter RA; *The Nature of True Virtue* (Boston 1765; reprinted in *Ethical Writings*,
ed. Paul Ramsey [New Haven: Yale University Press, 1989]), hereafter TV; and *History of the Work of Redemption* (Edinburgh, 1774; reprint, New Haven: Yale University Press, 1989), hereafter HR. The "Miscellaneous Observations" must be used
with caution. It was originally published in 1793 and consists of material from the
"Miscellanies." The editor (John Erskine) "took great liberties with the text, disre-
garded all chronological order, patched together widely separated excerpts, and
added whatever connections or conjunctions seemed appropriate to him"
(Townsend, *Philosophy of Edwards*, p. xi, n. 14).

the world" or that, if there is, it is not "properly an intelligent, volitive being" (Misc. 1298, T 218).

Even though Edwards thinks that reason *can* prove God's existence, determine the nature of many of His attributes, discern our obligations to Him, and establish the credibility of scripture, he believes that grace is needed both to help "the natural principles against those things that tend to stupefy it and to hinder its free exercise" (Misc. 626, T 111) and to "sanctify the reasoning faculty and assist it to see the clear evidence there is of the truth of religion in rational arguments" (Misc. 628, T 251).

In many respects, Edwards simply restates Puritan commonplaces. Although they conceded that "some of the things 'plainly proved' by scripture could also be detected by the 'light of natural reason,' " Puritans emphasized reason's powerlessness.[2] Robert Bolton, for instance, thought that if "a man looke upon Gods wayes onely with the eye of reason they are foolishnesse to him." Thomas Adams said, "there is no greater ods in the world than betweene our owne reason and God's wisdome." Peter Sterry maintained that "To seek out spiritual things by the scent and sagacity of reason were to plough with an Oxe and an Asse. . . . You cannot reach the things of reason by the hand of sense. . . . You cannot understand spirituall things Rationally. . . . Some say, that all truths which come by revelation of the Spirit, may also be demonstrated by Reason. But if they be, they are then no more Divine, but humane truths; They lose their certainty, beauty, efficacy; . . . Spirituall truths discovered by demonstrations of Reason, are like the Mistresse in her Cook-maid's clothes." According to the great Puritan divine William Perkins, one "must reject his owne naturall reason, and stoppe up the eyes of his naturall minde, like a blinde man, and suffer himselfe wholly to be guided by God's spirit in the things of God." And the Puritan mystic Francis Rous commended those who "have . . . quenched their owne naturall lamps, that they might get them kindled above by the Father of Lights."[3]

---

2. John Morgan, *Godly Learning; Puritan Attitudes towards Reason, Learning and Education* (Cambridge: Cambridge University Press, 1986), p. 51.

3. The quotations from Bolton, Adams, Perkins, and Rous are found in ibid., pp. 51–53. The quotation from Sterry is found in Geoffrey F. Nuttall, *The Holy*

As John Morgan points out, Puritan strictures on reason reflect the Reformed (and ultimately Augustinian and Pauline) insistence on human corruption. Reason is not exempt from the consequences of the Fall. Although natural reason may discover some truths about God (along with many errors), it is incapable of grasping His saving actions on our behalf. Puritan strictures also reflect their emphasis on an "experimental knowledge" of God's favor toward us. According to Arthur Dent, "the knowledge of the reprobate is like the knowledge which a mathematicall geographer hath of the earth and all the places in it, which is but a generall notion and a speculative comprehension of them. But the knowledge of the elect is like the knowledge of a traveller which can speake of experience and feeling, and hath beene there and seene and knowen the particulars."[4] Or, as William Baxter said;

> I do, therefore, neither despise evidence as unnecessary, nor trust to it alone as the sufficient total cause of my belief; for if God's grace do not open mine eyes, and come down in power upon my will, and insinuate into it a sweet acquaintance with the things unseen, and a taste of their goodness to delight my soul, no reasons will serve to stablish and comfort me, however undeniable soever; the way to have the firmest belief of the Christian faith, is to draw near and taste, and try it, and lay bare the heart to receive the impression of it, and then, by the sense of its admirable effects, we shall know that which bare speculation could not discover.[5]

Edwards shares these attitudes. What distinguishes him from other Puritan divines is not his learning or use of philosophical resources[6] but his philosophical acumen and the fact that the intellectual currents that most influenced him (continental rationalism and British

---

Spirit in Puritan Faith and Experience, 2d ed. (Chicago: University of Chicago Press, 1992), p. 37.

4. Quoted in Morgan, *Godly Learning*, p. 59.
5. Quoted in Nuttall, *Holy Spirit*, p. 47.
6. In spite of their strictures on reason, Puritans insisted on a learned clergy, and Puritan divines commonly drew on the ancient philosophers, the schoolmen, Ramus, and so on.

empiricism) are those that have both shaped modern philosophy and underlie the dominant view of rationality.

The following sections explore Edwards's position in detail. The first discusses his remarks on mystery and paradox and defends the claim that Edwards believed in the possibility of natural theology. The second examines his discussion of the sense of the heart, and the third shows why Edwards thought that grace is needed to reason properly.

The Possibility of Natural Theology

Edwards's remarks about mystery, paradox, and the impossibility of discovering spiritual truths do not preclude natural theology.

The inconsistencies Edwards alludes to, for instance, are only "*seeming* inconsistencies" and "*seeming* contradictions" (my emphases); they are not real ones. And the only sense in which theology is incomprehensible is that we lack "clear ideas of the things that are the subject of" its truths (Misc. 1100, T 213). We know *that* God necessarily exists, for example, but not *how* this can be true. Or we know "that the Godhead was united to man so as to be properly looked upon [as] the same person" but not "how it was effected" (Misc. 1340, T 234).[7]

But the most important point is this. "Paradox" and "incomprehensibility" also characterize other disciplines whose credentials are beyond dispute. Mathematical truths concerning "surd quantities and fluxions" are incomprehensible in the same sense, and "the reasonings and conclusions of the best metaphysicians and mathematicians concerning infinities are attended with paradoxes and seeming inconsistencies" (Misc. 1100, T 213; Misc. 1340, T 230). Philosophy provides other examples. Reason cannot "comprehend, or explain, or show, or conceive of any way that" minds and bodies can interact although it is obvious that they do (Misc. 1340, T 222). And when we attempt to formulate idealism (which Edwards believes to be both true and demonstrable), "we have got so far beyond those

---

7. At one point, Edwards glosses "inconsistent" and "incomprehensible" as (merely) "contrary to what would be expected" (Misc. 1340, T 232).

things for which language was chiefly contrived, that *unless we use extreme caution* we cannot speak . . . without literally contradicting ourselves" (Mind 355, my emphasis).

Paradoxes attend these disciplines because they deal with matters remote from "the common business and vulgar affairs of life, things obvious to sense and men's direct view." Their subject matters are not "the objects and affairs which earthly language was made to express," and the truths they discern "are not agreeable to such notions . . . and ways of thinking that grow up with us and are connatural to us" (Misc. 1340, T 227–28). The difficulties that attend theology are no greater in kind (although greater in degree) than those attending other disciplines dealing with "high" and "abstract" matters. It would be as illegitimate to conclude that natural or revealed theology is impossible, then, as to conclude that mathematics or metaphysics are.

Edwards's remarks concerning the impossibility of knowing God apart from revelation should be treated with the same caution. The following is typical. If people are not "led by revelation and direct teaching into a right way of using their reason, in arguing from effects to causes, etc., they would remain forever in the most woeful doubt and uncertainty concerning the nature and the very being of God. This appears not only by the state of the heathen world . . . but also by what appears among those who in these late ages have renounced divine revelation, even the wisest and greatest of 'em," such as Hobbes, Toland, Shaftesbury, and Hume (Misc. 1297, T 214).

I believe that Edwards wishes to make two points. The first is that "uninstructed" reason is powerless; no one is capable of erecting the fabric of *any* discipline on his or her own. The second is that we are powerless to *discover* theological truths although reason can *demonstrate* the truth of (many of) them *after* they have been revealed. Neither implies the impossibility of natural theology.

Miscellany 1297 is instructive. "The state of the heathen world" and "what appears among . . . the wisest and greatest of" the modern "deistical writers" shows that men and women who are not "led by revelation and direct teaching" fall into error. But the deists' errors are greater than those made by people "before the Gospel." For the heathen philosophers did not despise the revelation they had "by tradition from their ancestors, the ancient founders of nations, or from the Jews, which led 'em to embrace many truths contained in the Scripture." Nor did they reject everything beyond their comprehension. The ancients were willing to learn from tradition and to accept truths they did not fully understand, because they did not "proceed in" the deists' "exceeding haughtiness and dependence on their own mere singular understanding, disdaining all dependence on teaching." Nor did they "proceed with" the deists' "enmity against moral and divine truth having not been so irritated by it" (T 214, 217–18).

Sound reasoning is a social product. It presupposes instruction in an intellectual tradition and membership in a community that shares it. Intellectual traditions include beliefs about a subject matter, methods for resolving problems concerning it, and shared values that guide the process of inquiry. Traditions are not static. Beliefs are dropped and added. Sometimes the community is forced to modify its values or revise its methods of investigation.[8] Contributions to this process, however, are normally restricted to those who have been initiated into the community and have thus mastered its intellectual traditions, employ its methods of inquiry, and share its values.[9] As Edwards remarks, "knowledge bears an exact proportion to instruction. Why [else] does the learned and well educated reason better than the mere citizen? . . . There is no fallacy more gross than to imagine reason, utterly untaught and undisciplined, capable of the same attainments in knowledge as reason well refined and instructed" (Misc. Obs. 186).

Contributions to science or philosophy, for example, are seldom made by outsiders. Isolated reason is impotent. If we stand aloof from the scientific or philosophical community and (relying only on our "own singular understandings") refuse to accept anything we have not worked out on our own or fully understood, we are not likely to contribute to science or philosophy, or even to understand

8. Consider, for example, the shift in interest from taxonomy and classification to developmental explanations that occurs between the eighteenth and nineteenth centuries or increasing refinements in sampling techniques.

9. See Basil Mitchell, *The Justification of Religious Belief* (London: Macmillan, 1973), chap. 7.

them. If we are also hostile to them, we are still less likely to do so. Why should religion be different? Why suppose that those who cut themselves off from the religious community and its intellectual traditions,[10] rely only on their own reasonings, refuse to accept anything they have not fully understood, and are indifferent to religion or hostile to it are likely to establish truths about God?

Viable religious traditions are unlike other intellectual traditions, however, in one important respect. They can only be inaugurated by God. "In ordinary articles of knowledge, our sense and experience furnish reason with ideas and principles to work on. . . . But in respect to God, it can have no right idea nor axiom to set out with, till he is pleased to reveal it" (Misc. Obs. 186). "That the ancient philosophers and wiser heathen had so good notions of God as they had seems to be much more owing to tradition, which originated from divine revelation, than from their own invention" (Misc. 1340, T 231–32). Revelation is needed because "the first principles of religion, being of a high and spiritual nature, are harder to be found out than those of any other science . . . the minds of men are gross and earthly, used to objects of sense; and all their depraved appetites and corrupt dispositions, which are by nature opposite to true religion, help to increase the natural weakness of their reason" (Misc. Obs. 193).

Nevertheless, "it is one thing" to "strike upon" a point, and quite another "to work out a demonstration of" it "once it is proposed" (Misc. Obs. 185). "It is very needful that God should declare unto mankind what manner of being he is," but reason "is sufficient to confirm such a declaration after it is given, and enable us to see its consistence, harmony, and rationality, in many respects" (Misc. Obs.

10. But *which* community? There is no agreement on paradigms. The situation in religion resembles the current state of the social sciences or the situation in the physical sciences in the sixteenth and early seventeenth centuries. (See Gary Gutting, "Paradigms and Hermeneutics: A Dialogue on Kuhn, Rorty, and the Social Sciences," *American Philosophical Quarterly* 21 [1984], 1–16.) Even in cases like these, however, a person is not likely to do good work if he or she stands aloof from *all* traditions or is hostile to *all* science. One should also consider the possibility (of which I am skeptical) that the world's religions are converging toward a single tradition or community that will incorporate earlier ones. (See John Hick and Wilfred Cantwell Smith on this point.) Edwards assumes that the Christian tradition is paradigmatic. If it is, the analogy is strengthened.

217). "After once suggested and delivered," God's declarations are seen to be "agreeable to reason" (Misc. 1340, T 232). That there is only one God, for example, "is what we, now the gospel has so taught us, can see to be truth by our own reason . . . it can easily be shown by reason to be demonstrably true" (*HR* 398–99).

What Edwards denies is that correct ideas of God would have occurred to us if humanity had been left to its own devices. Whether this is true or not[11] is irrelevant to the possibility of natural theology. For the process of discovery is *in general* nonrational. (There are no rational procedures for discovering illuminating new scientific hypotheses, for example, or perspicacious interpretations of literary texts.) Whatever their origins, reason has ideas of God. Having them, it can show that they are not fictions; the truths of natural religion (that God exists, that He is sovereign, righteous, and so on) are demonstrable.

Natural reason can also ascertain that scripture is God's revelation and, knowing this, it can learn truths it could not acquire in other ways.

"Divine testimony" cannot be opposed to reason, evidence, or argument because it is a *rule* of reason, a *kind* of evidence, and a *type* of argument like the "human testimony of credible eye-witnesses," "credible history," "memory," "present experience," "geometrical mensuration," "arithmetical calculation," and "strict metaphysical distinction and comparison" (Misc. Obs. 228).[12] The statement that

11. Could not human beings *construct* the idea of God? Is it not probable that (as Hume, Feuerbach, and Freud argued) a weak, needy, and frightened humanity would invent ideas of supernatural beings? Edwards would undoubtedly agree with Calvin and Barth. Without supernatural assistance, the mind only manufactures idols—magnified images of itself, projections of its own hopes and fears. Edwards's criterion of idolatry would, of course, be the extent to which an idea of God conforms to Christian revelation. A nontheological (and possibly more persuasive) version of his argument might be this: Religious ideas cannot be adequately explained without appealing to religious experiences that are sui generis (Otto's numinous feelings, for example, or mystical experiences), or, more strongly, they cannot be adequately explained without appealing to *veridical* religious experiences.

12. Edwards does not clearly distinguish between evidence, argument, and rule of reason. The distinction is presumably this: Apparent memories are a type of evidence, justifying claims by appealing to memory is a type of argument, and the appropriate rule is "One's memories are normally reliable." Similarly, the contents of scripture are a type of evidence, justifying claims by appealing to scripture is a type of argument, and the appropriate rule is "Scripture is trustworthy."

"Scripture is reliable" resembles such rules as "The testimony of our senses may be depended on," "The agreed testimony of all we see and converse with continually is to be credited," and "The testimony of history and tradition is to be depended on, when attended with such and such credible circumstances" (Misc. 1340, T 221). Principles such as these can be established, or at least certified, by reason[13] and then used to establish other truths that cannot be established without their help ("Fire engines are red," for example, or "Christ atoned for our sins").

That reason can be appropriately used to assess the credentials of a rule of reasoning does not imply that opinions formed by a reason that does not employ the rule can be used to determine the truth or falsity of opinions established *by* its means. The naked eye, for example, "determines the goodness and sufficiency" of the optic glass, yet it would be absurd for a person to "credit no representation made by the glass, wherein the glass differs from his eye" and to refuse to believe, "that the blood consists partly of red particles and partly of limpid liquor because it all appears red to the naked eye" (Misc. Obs. 227). It would be equally absurd to reject truths that can be established by a reason that employs the rule "Memories are generally reliable" because what memory reports cannot be established by a reason that does not. It is just as unreasonable to discount what can be discovered by a reason that employs the rule that scripture is credible on the grounds that truths learned in this way cannot be established by a reason that rejects it.[14]

13. Edwards says, for example, that "general propositions" such as "Memory is dependable" "can be known only by reason" (Misc. 1340, T 220). Unfortunately, he does not explain *how* reason knows them. Are there arguments? Are the rules expressions of something like Hume's natural beliefs or Reid's inborn belief dispositions? Does the answer differ from case to case? One test of a rule's rationality is whether the results of applying it agree with the results of applying other rules. A check on the credibility of sense experience, for example, is "the agreement of the testimonies of the senses with other criteria of truth" (Misc. Obs. 230).

14. Edwards does not discuss instances of apparent conflict—cases in which the results of appropriately applying a rule conflict with the results of appropriately applying others. For example, we sometimes discount memory when it conflicts with the testimony of others. Or testimony is rejected when it conflicts with our perceptual experience. We presumably use some (rough) hierarchy of rules to adjudicate conflicts of this kind. We also refine rules as a result of experience. We learn, for example, when memory is reliable and when it is not. Of special interest are cases in

Although this passage does not explain *how* "Scripture is credible" can be established or certified, what Edwards has in mind is reasonably clear. The strongest evidence for scripture's divine authority is its spiritual beauty—a feature that natural reason cannot detect. Only those with converted hearts can perceive, taste, and relish the stamp of divine splendor on scripture and thus be *certain* of its teachings. (More on this shortly.) The unsanctified are nonetheless capable of acquiring a *probable* conviction of their truth. Scripture's authority is certified by miracles and fulfilled prophecy, the harmony between revealed and natural religion, scripture's beneficial effect on morality, and so on.[15] "None will doubt," says Edwards, "but that some natural men do yield a kind of assent . . . to the truths of the Christian religion, from the rational proofs or arguments that are offered to evince it" (*RA* 295). Probabilistic arguments for the truth of the gospel can be drawn from history, and "lately . . . these . . . have been set in a clear and convincing light" by the "learned" (*RA* 305). By exercising its natural faculties, reason can know that scripture is God's declaration and can therefore use "Scripture is reliable" as a rule to extend its knowledge.

Natural reason is thus capable of establishing the authority of scripture as well as the truths of natural religion. Why, then, does it so often find it difficult to do so? Not because the *evidence* is not obvious enough. Because these truths nearly concern us, God would not be good if He had not clearly declared them[16] (*OS* 155–57). We have sufficient "means of knowledge," therefore, as well as "a sufficient capacity" (*OS* 148). What is lacking is "a disposition to improve" the "light" God has given us (*OS* 149).

----

which scripture appears to conflict with the results of applying rules such as "The testimony of history and tradition is to be depended on" (the question of the historicity of *Daniel* or *Esther*, for example) or the results of employing "strict metaphysical distinction and comparison." Edwards thinks that conflicts like these are only apparent and undoubtedly believes that "Scripture is reliable" takes precedence over other rules. Nevertheless, one wishes that he had discussed the issue more thoroughly.

15. These arguments were commonly employed in the eighteenth century. For one of the better examples, see Samuel Clarke's *A Discourse concerning the Unchangeable Obligations of Natural Religion and the Truth and Certainty of the Christian Revelation* (London, 1706), especially Propositions VII–XV.

16. That the evidence is intrinsically clear is confirmed by the fact that it seems clear when the scales of sin are removed from our eyes.

The following two sections examine the ways in which grace repairs our damaged dispositions. The role that moral and spiritual virtues play in sound reasoning about divine matters will become evident as we proceed.

The Sense of the Heart

Jonathan Edwards is well known for his insistence on a "practical," or "experimental," religion that engages the human heart. At its core is a sense of God's excellence and loveliness, or of the beauty and splendor of divine things.

The savingly converted enjoy "gracious discoveries" of "God, in some of his sweet and glorious attributes manifested in the gospel, and shining forth in the face of Christ"—for example, "the all-sufficiency of the mercy and grace of God" or "the infinite power of God, and his ability to save them. . . . In some, the truth and certainty of the Gospel in general is the first joyful discovery they have. . . . More frequently Christ is distinctly made the object of the mind, in his all-sufficiency and willingness to save sinners" (*FN* 171).[17] Recalling his own conversion, Edwards says:

> The first instance that I remember of that sort of inward, sweet delight in God and divine things that I have lived much in since, was on reading those words, I Tim. i. 17. *Now unto the King eternal, immortal, invisible, the only wise God, be honor and glory for ever and ever, Amen.* As I read the words, there came into my soul, and was as it were diffused through it, a sense of the glory of the Divine Being; a new sense, quite different from any thing I ever experienced before. Never any words of scripture seemed to me as these words did. I thought with myself, how excellent a Being that was,

17. Edwards's discussions of the sense of the heart are located in *The Nature of True Virtue* and the "Miscellanies." For other relevant material, see *A Faithful Narrative of the Surprising Work of God, in the Conversion of Many Hundred Souls . . .* , and *The Distinguishing Marks of a Work of the Spirit of God* (respectively, Boston, 1737; Boston 1741; both reprinted in *The Great Awakening*, ed. C. C. Goen [New Haven: Yale University Press, 1972]), hereafter *FN* and *DM*, respectively; "A Divine and Supernatural Light"; "The Mind"; and "Personal Narrative" (*Jonathan Edwards: Representative Selections*, ed. Clarence H. Faust and Thomas H. Johnson [New York: American Book Co., 1935]), hereafter *PN*.

and how happy I should be, if I might enjoy that God, and be rapt up to him in heaven, and be as it were swallowed up in him for ever! (PN 59).

Again, Edwards tells us, "I remember the thoughts I used then to have of holiness. . . . It appeared to me, that there was nothing in it but what was ravishingly lovely; the highest beauty and amiableness . . . a *divine* beauty; far purer than anything here upon earth" (PN 63). "God," he says, "has appeared to me a glorious and lovely Being, chiefly on account of his holiness. . . . The doctrines of God's absolute sovereignty, and free grace, in showing mercy to whom he would show mercy; and man's absolute dependence on the operations of God's Holy Spirit, have very often appeared to me as sweet and glorious doctrines. These doctrines have been much my delight" (PN 67).

Some express their new experiences by the terms "sight or discovery," others by "a lively or feeling sense of heart" (*FN* 171–72). Both expressions refer to a new understanding of spiritual notions. Those who have these experiences find that phrases such as "a spiritual sight of Christ," "faith in Christ," "poverty of spirit," and so on, had not previously conveyed "those special and distinct ideas to their minds which they were intended to signify; in some respects no more than the names of colors are to convey the ideas to one that is blind from birth" (*FN* 174). But now "things of religion" seem "new to them . . . preaching is a new thing . . . the bible is a new book" (*FN* 181). Indeed, "the light and comfort which some of them enjoy . . . causes all things about 'em to appear as it were beautiful, sweet and pleasant to them: all things abroad, the sun, moon and stars, the clouds and sky, the heavens and earth, appear as it were with a cast of divine glory and sweetness upon them" (*FN* 183).

This section examines Edwards's attempt to make philosophical and theological sense of these experiences. It is divided into six parts. The first two discuss the nature of the idea of spiritual beauty and Edwards's reasons for thinking that our apprehension of beauty is a kind of sensation or perception. The third explores the implications of Edwards's theory for the epistemic status of religious belief, and the fourth and fifth examine his defense of the objectivity of the new "spiritual sense." The last part explores the bearing of Edwards's remarks on current discussions.

A New Simple Idea

The objects of a sense or feeling of the heart are (1) "actual [i.e., lively, clear, and distinct] ideas," (2) of things pertaining to the will or affections, (3) that involve a "feeling of sweetness or pleasure, or of bitterness or pains." They include (the ideas of)[18] (1) "beauty and deformity," "good or evil," as well as "excellency," "value," "importance" and their opposites, (2) delight and pleasure and pain and misery, (3) affective and conative attitudes, dispositions, and states ("desires and longings, esteem . . . hope, fear, contempt, choosing, refusing . . . loving, hating, anger," (4) "dignity," "terrible greatness, or awful majesty," "meanness or contemptibleness," and so on, and (5) the nonevaluative characteristics on which beauty and deformity, pleasure and pain, and attributes such as dignity or majesty depend.[19] The object of a sense or feeling of the heart is, in essence, good and evil, and what pertains to it. Natural good or evil is "good or evil which is agreeable or disagreeable to human nature as such." Spiritual good or evil is what is agreeable or disagreeable to people with "spiritual frames," that is, to those who, because the Spirit dwells within them, love being in general (i.e., God and the beings that derive from Him, are absolutely dependent on Him, and reflect Him) (Misc. 782, T 113–26).

The "immediate object of this spiritual sense" is "the beauty of holiness" (RA 260), "the spiritual excellency, beauty, or sweetness of divine things" (Misc. 782), "true moral or spiritual beauty" (TV 548), "the highest and primary beauty" (TV 561)—a "new simple idea" that cannot be produced by the "exalting, varying or compounding of that kind of perceptions or sensations which the mind had before" (RA 205).

18. Edwards believes that the immediate objects of mental acts are ideas. Like Berkeley, he tends to conflate ideas and their contents (what the ideas are ideas *of*).

19. Why regard these as objects of a sense or feeling of the heart? Presumably because (for example) a perception of beauty or importance involves a perception of the nonevaluative features on which beauty or importance depend, or because one cannot fully grasp or understand these nonevaluative properties without perceiving their beauty or importance, or both.

What kind of idea is this? Or, put another way, what does Edwards mean by "(true) beauty?" His remarks are open to at least three interpretations: that (1) "beauty" refers to the delight or pleasure that holy things evoke in people with spiritual "frames" or "tempers," (2) "beauty" refers to a dispositional property, the tendency of holy things to produce this pleasure or delight in the converted, and (3) "beauty" designates a love of being in general, that is, the consent of being to being that holiness consists in.

There is some evidence that Edwards held the first or second view. He asserts, for example, that "That form or quality is called 'beautiful,' . . . the view or idea of which is immediately pleasant to the mind . . . this agreeableness or gratefulness of the idea is what is called beauty . . . we come by the idea or sensation of beauty . . . by immediate sensation of the gratefulness of the idea [thing] called 'beautiful' " (*TV* 619). In "The Mind" 1 (332) Edwards assimilates beauty and excellence and then says, "We would know, why proportion is more excellent than disproportion, that is, why proportion is pleasant to the mind and disproportion unpleasant." Passages such as these imply that beauty is some kind of pleasure or agreeableness,[20] or a tendency to produce it in appropriate circumstances.

We probably should not attribute the second (dispositional) view to Edwards. If "(true) beauty" referred to the tendency to produce a unique sort of delight in those with spiritual frames, the idea of beauty would be a complex idea or "mixed mode."[21] This conflicts with the claim that spiritual beauty is a new simple idea (*RA* 205).[22]

20. Edwards clearly thinks that there are qualitative differences between pleasures. The pleasure that the natural man takes in secondary beauty (i.e., in "regularity, order, uniformity, symmetry, proportion, harmony, etc." [*TV* 561–62]) is qualitatively different from the spiritual person's delight in holiness.

21. Locke's mixed modes are a species of complex ideas. Roughly, a mixed mode is an idea of a set of properties that cannot subsist by itself. (Ideas of substances, therefore, are not mixed modes.)

22. This is not absolutely decisive. In Locke's view, "red" can be used to refer not only to a simple sensation but also to a power of producing this sensation that certain objects possess in virtue of their primary qualities; that is, "red" can be used to express a mixed mode as well as a simple idea. I will argue that Edwards's use of "beauty" exhibits a similar ambiguity. Nevertheless, it is reasonably clear that Locke believed that, in its primary sense, "red" denotes a simple idea and that Edwards thought the same of "beauty."

There are also problems in attributing the first view to Edwards. The philosophers who most influenced Edwards (Locke and the Cartesians) explicitly denied that ideas of pleasure and pain tell us anything about the nature of the objects that produce them.[23] The idea of true beauty does. Edwards explicitly rejects the suggestion that "the idea we obtain by this spiritual sense could in no respect be said to be a knowledge or perception of anything besides what was in our own minds," or that it is "no representation of anything without." On the contrary, the idea of spiritual beauty is "the representation and image of the moral perfection and excellency of the Divine Being . . . of which we could have no true idea without it" (TV 622–23).[24]

A more compelling reason for doubting that Edwards identified beauty with pleasure (or a tendency to produce it) is that he so often speaks as if it were an *objective* property of the things that have it. One of Edwards's central theses is that God's nature and activity are overwhelmingly beautiful, and that the spiritual and natural beauty of creatures is a reflection of, or participation in, God's own beauty. The tenor of passages expressing these claims seems inconsistent with the suggestion that beauty is no more than a sensation which holy things produce in the suitably disposed (or a power to produce it). Edwards was strongly influenced by Locke and other empiricists. But he also belongs to a Puritan tradition that contains an important Platonic strand.[25] It may therefore be significant that Platonism thinks of beauty as an objective property.

Finally, a number of texts appear to identify beauty with the consent of being to being. This, too, seems inconsistent with the notion that beauty is some sort of pleasure or delight.

23. See Locke, *Human Understanding* (hereafter *HU*) 2.8. See also Hutcheson who says that moral approbation (i.e., the disinterested delight in morally good actions and dispositions) "cannot be supposed an image of anything external, more than the pleasures of harmony, of taste, of smell" (*Illustrations on the Moral Sense* [Cambridge: Harvard University Press, 1971], p. 164, hereafter *Illustrations*).

24. This point is inconclusive, however, because Edwards sometimes departs from Locke. For example, he asserts that beauty is a simple idea although Locke thought it was a mixed mode (*HU* 2.12.51).

25. Edwards was influenced by Henry More (who self-consciously combined Platonism and Cartesianism). He was also familiar with Ralph Cudworth and John Smith and quotes both with approval.

In "The Mind" 1, for example, Edwards assimilates beauty and excellency and then says, "excellency *consists in* the similarities of one being to another—not merely equality and proportion, but any kind of similarness. . . . This is an universal *definition* of excellency: The consent of being to being, or being's consent to entity" (336, my emphasis). Edwards continues to speak this way in later works. He says, for example, that "the true beauty and loveliness of all intelligent beings does primarily and most essentially *consist in* their moral excellency or holiness," that is, in their benevolence or love of being in general. "Holiness *is* . . . the beauty of the divine nature" (*RA* 257, my emphasis; cf. 258–59). In *The Nature of True Virtue*, Edwards asserts that true benevolence "is the thing wherein true moral or spiritual beauty primarily *consists*. Yea, spiritual beauty *consists wholly in* this and in" what proceeds from it (*TV* 648, my emphasis). "There is [also] another, inferior, secondary beauty, which is some image of this . . . which *consists in* a mutual consent and agreement of different things, in form, manner, quantity, and visible end or design; called by the various names of regularity, order, uniformity, symmetry, proportion, harmony, etc." (*TV* 561, my emphasis). Passages of this kind imply that beauty just *is* (i.e., is identical with) some kind of agreement. Primary or spiritual beauty is one and the same thing as benevolence or the "consent or agreement, or union of being to being," and secondary beauty is identical with symmetry, harmony, or proportion, that is, "uniformity in the midst of variety" (*TV* 561–62).

But there are also serious objections to *this* interpretation. Edwards often speaks as if beauty were a property *of* holiness and hence not the *same* thing as holiness. In the *Religious Affections*, for example, he speaks of "the loveliness of the moral excellency of divine things . . . the beauty and sweetness of their moral excellency" (253 f.), "the beauty of their moral excellency," "the beauty of his holiness," "the beauty of his moral attributes" (256), "the loveliness of divine things . . . viz., . . . the beauty of their moral perfection" (271), "the beauty of the moral perfection of Christ" (273), "the beauty of holiness, or true moral good" (274), and so on. Edwards also asserts that the unconverted can see everything that pertains to God's and the saints' moral attributes *except* their "beauty and amiableness" (*RA* 264), thus implying some sort of distinction between these attributes and their beauty. Finally, beauty is a *simple* idea. The consent of (conscious) being to being, however, is complex.[26]

In short, there is textual evidence for the claim that Edwards identified true beauty with a spiritual sensation or a tendency to produce it and also for the claim that he identified it with consent. Both views appear incompatible with some of Edwards's other positions. The first seems inconsistent with his belief that the apprehension of beauty is a "perception" of something existing "without" the mind, and the second is inconsistent with his conviction that beauty is a simple idea. Can a coherent position be constructed from Edwards's remarks? He may have been driving at this: Beauty is identical with benevolence or agreement in somewhat the same way in which water is identical with H_2O or in which (according to materialists) consciousness is identical with certain arrangements of matter. (This accommodates the fact that one can perceive benevolence or agreement without perceiving its beauty even though its beauty "consists in" benevolence or agreement.) But benevolence is also the "objective" or "physical" basis of a dispositional property (the tendency to produce a new simple idea in those with converted hearts). The new idea is a delight or pleasure in being's consent to being which somehow "represents" or is a "perception of" it.

On this interpretation, the idea of true beauty resembles Locke's ideas of primary and secondary qualities. Spiritual delight is, in Locke's words, a simple "sensation or perception in our understanding" like our ideas of color or solidity. (*HU* 2.8.8). The dispositional property is what Locke calls a "quality," a "power to produce those ideas in us" (ibid.). Benevolence is the objective configuration underlying this power and corresponds to the microstructure of bodies that underlie their tendency to excite ideas of primary and secondary qualities in minds like ours. Like simple ideas of primary and secondary qualities, the new spiritual sensation "represents" or is a

---

26. Of course, Edwards *might* have believed that the relevant relational terms ("consents," "is equal to," "agrees with," "harmonizes with," etc.) stand for simple ideas, but he never says this, and although Locke thinks that the ideas of relations "*terminate* in simple ideas" (arise from the comparison of simple ideas), he does not seem to think that relations themselves are simple ideas (*HU* 2.25.9–10; 2.28.18–20).

"perception" of its object. Just as "extension" or "red" can refer to the idea, the power, or the physical configuration that is the base of the power, so "beauty" can refer to the sensation, to the relevant dispositional property, or to benevolence. (My interpretation thus accounts for the ambiguity of Edwards's remarks.)[27]

Edwards's account of spiritual perception is subject to some of the same difficulties as Locke's account of sense perception.[28] Is it, in any way, *less* satisfactory? It may be in one respect. If I am right, the idea of true beauty is a kind of delight or relish and *also* an apparent cognition. *Can* something be both? It is not sufficient to argue that perceptions of objectively real value properties can be inherently affective (and thus pleasurable or painful), for Edwards does not think of pleasure and pain in this way. Pleasures and pains are not qualities or affective dimensions of more complex experiences. They are discrete internal sensations. But if spiritual pleasure *is* a kind of internal delight or thrill, how can it *also* be a true representation of something existing without? Ordinary pleasures and pains differ from visual or auditory impressions in lacking what Berkeley called "outness"; they do not seem to point beyond themselves. Either spiritual pleasure is unlike ordinary pleasure in this respect, or it is not an apparent cognition.

In the next subsection we will see *why* Edwards calls the feeling of spiritual pleasure a "perception." Whether this resolves the difficulty, however, is doubtful.

Spiritual Sensing

Even though the spiritual sense is closely connected with a person's will or inclination,[29] it is a cognitive faculty—"a new founda-

27. Does the idea of beauty not only "represent" but also "resemble" its object, as Locke's ideas of extension, figure and motion "resemble" the objective configurations that cause them? Edwards never explicitly says it does. (That the idea is a "perception" of "something without" only distinguishes it from ideas of tertiary qualities.) In calling it "knowledge," however, and in insisting that we can have no true idea of its object without it, Edwards implies that the idea *accurately* represents (some aspect of) its object. This suggests that the idea of beauty should be assimilated to Locke's ideas of primary qualities.

28. It is not clear that the mind's immediate objects are ideas, how they represent or resemble their objects, and so on.

29. At one point, Edwards asks, "concerning speculative understanding and

tion laid in the nature of the soul, for a new kind of exercises of the
. . . faculty of *understanding*" (*RA* 206, my emphasis).[30] A sense of the
heart involves a person's will or inclination because "when the mind
is sensible" of spiritual beauty "that implies a sensibleness of sweetness and delight in the presence of the idea of it", "the mind . . . relishes and feels." But "there is [also] the nature of instruction in it"; it
is a "kind of understanding" (*RA* 272).

Why does Edwards speak of this new cognition as a kind of perception or sensation? Partly because the idea of a spiritual sense was a
Puritan commonplace. For example, John Owen said that God
"gives . . . a spirituall sense, a Taste of the things themselves upon the
mind, Heart and Conscience." According to Richard Sibbes, "It is
knowledge with a taste . . . God giveth knowledge *per modum gus-
tus.*" Francis Rous said that "after we have tasted those heavenly
things . . . from this taste there ariseth a new, but a true, lively, and
experimental knowledge of the things so tasted. . . . For even in natural fruits there are certain relishes . . . which nothing but the taste it
self can truly represent and shew unto us. The West-Indian Piney
[pineapple] cannot be so expressed in words, even by him that hath
tasted it, that he can deliver over the true shape and character of that
taste to another that hath not tasted it."[31] Edwards was indebted to
his predecessors for the idea of a spiritual sensation. His development
of that concept, however, is heavily influenced by empiricists such as
Locke and (possibly) Hutcheson.[32]

---

sense of heart; whether any difference between the sense of the heart and the will
or inclination" (Subjects 14).

30. Cf. *RA* 275. It involves a new "sort of *understanding* or *knowledge* . . . [viz.]
that *knowledge* of divine things from whence all truly gracious affections do proceed"
(my emphasis).

31. The quotations are from Nuttall, *Holy Spirit*, pp. 39, 139.

32. Locke was a major influence. Hutcheson's *Inquiry into the Original of our Ideas
of Beauty and Virtue* (London: 1725; hereafter *Inquiry*) is referred to in Edwards's "Catalogue of Books" on p. 8 and p. 22. On p. 22, Edwards writes, "Hutcheson's Essay on
the Passions cited in his Enquiry into the Original of our Ideas of Beauty and
Virtue," which implies that he had read the *Inquiry* by that time. (Thomas H. Johnson ["Jonathan Edwards's Background of Reading," *Publications of the Colonial Society
of Massachusetts* 28 (1930–33), 194–222] estimates that pages 15–43 date from 1746 to
1757.) Hutcheson is mentioned three times in *True Virtue*, and quotations from the *Inquiry* occur in *Original Sin* on pages 225 and 226. Hutcheson's *An Essay on the Nature
and Conduct of the Passions and Affections* and *Illustrations on the Moral Sense* (two essays)

The object of the spiritual sense is a new simple idea, and Edwards shared Locke's conviction that simple ideas come "from experience" (*HU* 2.1.2). As Francis Hutcheson said, "Reasoning or intellect seems to raise no new species of ideas but [only] to discover or discern the relation of" ideas "received by some immediate powers of perception internal or external which we may call sense" (*Illustrations* 135).

Spiritual understanding also involves a kind of relish or delight, and Edwards follows Locke and Hutcheson in thinking that being pleased or pained, like a feeling of tactual pressure or being appeared to redly, is a kind of sensation or perception. (All three believe that pleasure and pain are simple ideas.)

Then again, the new simple idea occurs involuntarily, and Edwards associates sensation with passivity (cf. Subjects 29). This too was a commonplace. For example, Hutcheson said that a sense is "a determination of the mind to receive any idea from the presence of an object . . . independent on our will" (*Inquiry*, Second Treatise, I, I).

Finally, the mind's apprehension of true or spiritual beauty is immediate (noninferential). As Edwards says, "this manner of being affected with the" beauty of a thing "depends not . . . on any reasonings . . . but on the frame of our minds whereby they are so made that" as soon as we perceive or cognize it, it "appears beautiful" (*TV* 619).[33] A comparison with Hutcheson is again instructive, for Hutcheson argued that the power of receiving the idea of beauty should be called a "sense" because "we are struck at the first with the beauty" (*Inquiry*, Second Treatise, I, XII).

It is thus clear *why* Edwards speaks of the new cognition as a perception or sensation. Whether he should have done so is another matter.

---

appeared in 1728 (three years after the first edition of the *Inquiry*). This work is entered in the "Catalogue" on pages 22 and 32. In the "Book of Controversies," the *Nature and Conduct of the Passions* "is quoted, and this passage is incorporated into *Original Sin* but credited to Turnbull" (Clyde A. Holbrook, "Introduction," *OS* 74–75). The implication is that Edwards was familiar with the two essays. Whether he was significantly influenced by Hutcheson, though, is unclear.

33. Cf. *Religious Affections*, 281–82, where Edwards speaks of the immediacy with which this new sense judges of the spiritual beauty of actions. See also *The Nature of True Virtue*, pp. 619–20.

There is little force in the third and fourth considerations. Our sensations (and the beliefs directly based on them) appear involuntary and immediate, but so too does our recognition of the fact that $2 + 2 = 4$. Passivity and immediacy are not peculiar to ideas derived from (internal or external) sensation.

The first two considerations carry more weight. Locke and Hutcheson identify reason with reasoning. Reason is sharply distinguished from the will and its affections and from the senses. Its sole function is to manipulate ideas received from other sources. Edwards shares these views.[34] Reason does not have an affective dimension and is not the source of new simple ideas. The cognition of true beauty, on the other hand, *has* an affective dimension since it involves relish or delight. Furthermore, its object is a new simple idea. Spiritual cognition must therefore be some kind of sensation or perception.

This conclusion seems inconsistent with other aspects of Edwards's position. A number of Hutcheson's critics took exception to his moral sense theory because they believed that (1) at least some moral propositions are necessarily true, and (2) necessary truths are discerned by reason.[35] Hutcheson maintained that the moral sense grasps the goodness of benevolent actions and dispositions, that is, perceives that benevolence is (morally) good. His critics objected that "benevolence is good" is necessarily true and that necessary truths are apprehended by *reason*. It is therefore significant that Edwards, too, apparently believed that moral truths are necessary.[36] Nor is he likely to have thought that the connection between benevolent actions and dispositions and spiritual beauty is only contingent—that holiness or benevolence might not have

34. "If we take *reason* strictly—not for the faculty of mental perception in general [which would include sense perception], but for ratiocination . . . the perceiving of spiritual beauty and excellency no more belongs to reason, than it belongs to the sense of feeling to perceive colors. . . . Reason's work is to perceive truth and not excellency" (DSL 18).

35. See, for example, the correspondence between Hutcheson and Gilbert Burnet.

36. Edwards clearly thinks that at least some moral truths are necessary. See *Freedom of the Will* (Boston, 1754; reprint, New Haven: Yale University Press, 1957), p. 153. Edwards's example is, "It is . . . fit and suitable, that men should do to others, as they would that they should do to them." It is worth observing that Locke, too, thinks that moral truths are necessary (*HU* 3.11.15–18; 4.3.18–20; and 4.4.7–10.)

been truly beautiful. But if "holiness is beautiful" *is* necessarily true, Edwards seems committed to the view that our knowledge of at least some necessary truths is derived from a sense, that is, that some necessary truths are perceived by a kind of sensation. And this is not plausible.

One *may* be able to apprehend the redness of a table without apprehending *that* the table is red. (Perhaps animals and infants do.) But *can* one apprehend the moral goodness of a benevolent action without apprehending *that* the action is morally good or apprehend its spiritual beauty without apprehending *that* it is truly beautiful? This seems doubtful. The idea of beauty derives from experience in the sense that one acquires it by encountering beautiful objects. But the idea of beauty does not seem to be a discrete feeling or sensation (like a feeling of sexual pleasure or a raw sensation of redness) that is *first* received from experience and *then* incorporated in a judgment. On the contrary, receiving the idea of beauty appears to *be* judging that what one is contemplating is beautiful. Edwards seems committed to claiming that this judgment is necessarily true. Does it make any sense, then, to speak of a person's apprehension of a thing's beauty as some kind of internal or external sensing?

If one were to interpret spiritual cognition as an "intellectual intuition" with affective overtones, one could avoid this problem as well as that raised at the end of the last subsection. Spiritual "perception" would then be something like our immediate recognition of the prima facie rightness of an instance of justice or kindness on a view like W. D. Ross's. Edwards was familiar with at least one account of this type, that of the Cambridge Platonist John Smith.

Like Edwards, Smith insisted on the inadequacy of a merely notional or intellectual understanding of spiritual things. He, too, thought that divine truths can only be understood by those who lead holy lives, and he, too, spoke of a "spiritual sensation." "The soul," said Smith, "itself hath its sense, as well as the body: and therefore David . . . calls not for speculation but sensation, Taste and see how good the Lord is." But Smith's spiritual sensation is an act of "that reason that is within us . . . [the] eye of the soul . . . our intellectual faculty." This intellectual intuition or perception of reason *incorporates* love or delight but is not identical with them.[37] (Smith does not find this problematic because he shares the Platonic view that reason itself has an affective dimension. Knowing the good involves loving it and delighting in it).[38]

A view such as Smith's sidesteps the two problems confronting Edwards—how a feeling of delight can also be an apparent cognition, and how a necessary truth can be grasped by a kind of sensation. Edwards's commitment to empiricism precluded this solution. Philosophers such as Locke identified reason with ratiocination and insisted that simple ideas originate in experience (internal or external sensation). Because Edwards accepted these theses, he could not construe spiritual cognitions as rational intuitions. Whether they are essential to his epistemology, however, is debatable.[39]

The Cognition of Spiritual Truths

Although the spiritual sense's direct object is true beauty or excellency, it also has an indirect object—spiritual facts or truths. There are two cases to consider.

In the first, the spiritual sense enables us to recognize the truth of propositions that are logically or epistemically related to the excellency of divine things. For example: Our apprehension of Christ's beauty and excellency produces a conviction of His sufficiency as a Mediator (Misc. 782, T 126; RA 273, 302). To grasp the appropriateness of God's end in creation, namely, the communication of His glory *ad extra*, one must perceive its beauty. An appreciation of the splendor of God's glory is also needed to comprehend the fitness of

37. The quotations are from Smith's "Of the True Way or Method of Attaining to Divine Knowledge," in *Select Discourses* (New York: Garland, 1978). (I have modernized the capitalization and spelling.) In his introduction to *Religious Affections*, John E. Smith denies that Smith's spiritual sensation is an intellectual intuition (RA 66). Quotations like the last, however, and the Platonic tenor of the discourse as a whole, seem to support my interpretation.

38. "Intellectual life, as [the Platonists] phrase it" is a nondiscursive "knowledge . . . [that] is always pregnant with divine virtue, which ariseth out of an happy union of souls with God, and is nothing else but a living imitation of a Godlike perfection drawn out by a strong fervent love of it. This divine knowledge . . . makes us amorous of divine beauty . . . and this divine love and purity, reciprocally exalts divine knowledge" (Smith, *Select Discourses*, p. 20).

39. For one thing (as John E. Smith and others have pointed out), the line between will and understanding is more flexible in Edwards than in Locke or Hutcheson.

the means He employs to secure it and thus understand His wisdom (*RA* 274, 302). Nor can one discern "the amiableness of the duties . . . that are required of us" unless one perceives the excellency of divine things (*RA* 274). Or again, one must see the beauty of holiness to appreciate the "hatefulness of sin" (*RA* 274, 301) and thus be convinced of the justice of divine punishment and our inability to make satisfaction (*RA* 302). The spiritual sense, then, enables us to grasp the truth of a number of important doctrines.

But it also helps us grasp the truth of the gospel scheme as a whole (*RA* 291–92). A conviction of the gospel's truth is an inference from the beauty or excellency of what it depicts, namely, "God and Jesus Christ . . . the work of redemption, and the ways and works of God" (DSL 8). "There is a divine and superlative glory in these things" that distinguishes "them from all that is earthly and temporal" (DSL 8). A spiritual person "truly sees" this glory (*RA* 298); his perception of it is as immediate and direct as a perception of color or the sweetness of food (DSL 18). (This was not, of course, a new idea. Thus, Richard Sibbes said, "God . . . causeth him to see a divine majesty shining forth in the scriptures, so that there must be an infused establishing by the Spirit to settle the heart in this first principle . . . that the Scriptures are the word of God." Or again, "How do you know the word to be the word? It carrieth proof and evidence in itself. It is an evidence that the fire is hot to him that feeleth it, and that the sun shineth to him that looks on it; how much more doth the word. . . . I am sure I felt it, it warmed my heart, and converted me.")[40]

A conviction of the gospel's truth "is an effect and natural consequence of this perception" (DSL 8). The perception and conviction are nonetheless distinct. The mind *infers* the truth and reality of the things the gospel contains from its *perception* of their spiritual beauty. There is, however, no "long chain of arguments; the argument is but one, and the evidence direct; the mind ascends to the truth of the gospel but by one step, and that is its divine glory" (*RA* 298–99; cf. Misc. 782, T 126).[41] Because only one step is involved, we can

40. Quoted in Nuttall, *Holy Spirit*, pp. 23, 39.

41. Presumably the argument is: (1) Gospel doctrines exhibit a divine excellency or beauty. Therefore, (2) Gospel doctrines are true. (2) follows from (1) *if* doctrines

truly say that the divinity, or reality, or truth of the gospel is "as it were" known intuitively, that "a soul may have a kind of intuitive knowledge of the divinity [or truth, or reality] of the things exhibited in the gospel" (RA 298).[42]

The mind's object differs in the two cases. In the first, it is a comparatively specific doctrinal proposition that is logically or epistemically connected with other propositions that affirm that some person or characteristic or activity or state of affairs is truly amiable or beautiful or excellent. Our spiritual sense enables us to *perceive* the truth of the latter and from this we *infer* the truth of the former. In the second, the mind's object is the content of the gospel as a whole—what Paul Ricoeur has called "the world of the text."[43] The central or controlling features of this world—God, Christ, and the scheme of salvation—are *perceived* to be truly beautiful. On the basis of this perception one immediately concludes that the biblical

---

that exhibit this supernatural radiance or splendor have a supernatural author. (On this point, see DSL 10; Misc. 256, T 249; and Misc. 782, T 126.) How is this generalization related to the argument? If the inference involves only one step, it cannot be functioning as a premise. Perhaps, then, the generalization is an inference rule. Or perhaps Edwards thinks of it as a necessary truth. (If it is, then [1] entails [2].) Or perhaps it is simply an inductive generalization from a set of "natural inferences"— judgments that the redeemed find themselves spontaneously making in the presence of the gospel and that are trustworthy given that their new faculties are God-given. (If the third alternative is correct, the generalization plays *no* role in the argument. The second and third interpretations seem most likely.)

42. A superficial reading of some passages might suggest that Edwards thinks that our knowledge of divine reality is immediate. Thus Miscellanies 201 (T 246–47) and 408 (T 249–50) assert that ideas that are clear and lively and cohere with each other and with other ideas are quite properly regarded as real or true. Those with converted hearts find the ideas of religion (scripture) clear, lively, internally coherent, and in harmony with their other ideas. They, therefore, quite properly take them to be real or true. But this "appearing real . . . cannot be drawn out into formal arguments." It depends on "ten thousand little relations and mutual agreements that are ineffable" "and is a sort of seeing rather than reasoning the truth of religion." But Edwards is not clearly denying that the conviction of reality is inferential. (He may simply be insisting on its psychological immediacy and coerciveness and on the fact that it does not rest on *formal* argument.) In any case, his normal view is that presented in "Divine and Supernatural Light" and *Religious Affections*, namely, that the reality of divine things is inferred by one step from their spiritual beauty and excellency.

43. Paul Ricoeur, "Philosophy and Religious Language," *Journal of Religion* 54 (1974), 71–85.

world is not fictional like those depicted in *The Brothers Karamazov* or *Moby-Dick*, but *real*.

Edwards's view has some interesting implications. If my interpretation is correct, the new spiritual sense does not involve a direct or immediate or quasi-perceptual awareness of God Himself. Instead, God's reality is *inferred* from the excellency and beauty of the things depicted in scripture. As we have seen, however, the inference "is without any long chain of arguments; the argument is but one, and the evidence direct." Because of the inference's spontaneity and immediacy, a person can even be said to have "a kind of intuitive knowledge" of divinity (*RA* 298). Edwards's interpretation of the redeemed's knowledge of God's reality thus resembles Descartes's and Locke's account of our knowledge of other minds and physical objects. These things are not directly perceived, but their reality or presence is spontaneously and immediately inferred from sensations or impressions that *are* directly apprehended. Edwards thinks our knowledge of God is similar. Although God is not *directly* perceived, His reality is no more remote or uncertain than other minds or physical objects are in Locke's view.

If I am right, Edwards's position differs from a basic beliefs approach. One's belief in God is not basic like our memory beliefs, or perceptual beliefs, or beliefs in simple necessary truths but is, instead, inferential. On the other hand, the inference on which one's belief is based does not involve a long or complicated chain of reasoning, and it is as spontaneous and compelling as our (alleged) inference to other minds or the reality of the physical world. The redeemed's belief in God is thus similar to some of Hume's natural beliefs—the belief in the continued existence of unperceived physical objects, for example, and (on some interpretations) the belief in a designer.[44] It differs in that the *basis* of the inference is a new simple idea that God bestows on the regenerate and because (in Edwards's opinion) the inference is *sound*.

---

44. Cf., for example, Ronald J. Butler, "Natural Belief and the Enigma of Hume," *Archiv für Geschichte der Philosophie* 42 (1960), 73–100, or John Hick, "A New Form of Theistic Argument," *Proceedings of the XIV International Congress of Philosophy* 5 (1970), 336–41. See also J. C. A. Gaskin, *Hume's Philosophy of Religion* (London Barnes and Noble, 1978), chap. 8.

The Objectivity of the Spiritual Sense

The final chapter of *The Nature of True Virtue* attempts to show that "the frame of mind, or inward sense . . . whereby the mind is disposed to" relish true virtue for its spiritual beauty, is not "given arbitrarily" but agrees "with the necessary nature of things" (*TV* 620). But the "frame of mind" that disposes a person to delight in true beauty (i.e., to be pleased with benevolence) is benevolence itself. Edwards concludes that it will be sufficient to show that *benevolence* agrees with the nature of things.

Edwards's strategy, in other words, is this. True benevolence is the mechanism underlying the new spiritual sense. If we can show that benevolence has a foundation in the nature of things, we can conclude that the spiritual sense, too, is aligned with reality. Edwards's task, then, is to prove that benevolence agrees with the "necessary nature of things." He has four arguments for this conclusion. The first two are unconvincing. The third and fourth are more persuasive.

Edwards's first argument is this:

1. A being with understanding and inclinations necessarily desires its own happiness (i.e., it desires what it wants or desires or finds agreeable).
2. Benevolence is the disposition to benefit being *in general*.
3. Therefore, a being with understanding and inclinations must approve of benevolence (for it benefits *him*). (From 1 and 2.)
4. Hence, if a being with understanding and inclinations approves of vice (i.e., of malevolence or indifference to being in general), then his attitudes are inconsistent. (From 3.)
5. Virtue (benevolence) can be approved without inconsistency.
6. If virtue (benevolence) can be approved without inconsistency and vice (malevolence or indifference) cannot, then virtue agrees with the nature of things and vice does not.
7. Therefore, virtue agrees with the nature of things and vice does not. (From 4, 5, and 6.) (*TV* 621–22).

The argument, if sound, shows that virtue agrees with the nature of things in the sense that loving virtue is a more rational (i.e., coherent) response to reality than loving vice.

But the proof is not persuasive. A person is not inconsistent in approving and disapproving (or not approving) of the same thing if he or she approves and disapproves (or fails to approve) of it in different respects. And this is surely the case here. The wicked approve of benevolence when it benefits them but hate it, or are indifferent toward it, when it benefits others. They approve of (or are indifferent to) malevolence or indifference when directed toward others but not when directed toward themselves. These attitudes may be reprehensible but they are not inconsistent. Let us therefore turn to Edwards's second argument:

1. Benevolence is "agreement or consent of being to being."
2. Being or "general existence" is the nature of things.
3. Therefore, benevolence agrees with the nature of things (*TV* 620). The argument establishes its conclusion by identifying the nature of things with what is (viz., being in general) and identifying agreement with being's consent to being.

This too seems unconvincing. Edwards's argument only establishes a tautology—that consent to being (i.e., benevolence) is consent to (i.e., agreement with) being (i.e., the nature of things). What *needs* to be shown is that benevolence or consent to being is an *appropriate* response to the nature of things, and his argument does not do this.

But this criticism, although correct, is superficial. For it neglects the argument's theistic context. Edwards believes that being in general is *God* and the "particular beings" that depend on Him and manifest His glory. A consent to, or love of, being in *this* sense is surely an appropriate response to it. The theistic metaphysics becomes explicit in Edwards's third argument.

1. God "is in effect being in general." (All being either is God or unconditionally depends on Him.)
2. It is "necessary, that God should agree with himself, be united with himself, or love himself."
3. Therefore, God is necessarily benevolent. (From 1 and 2—in loving Himself, God loves "being in general" and is therefore benevolent.)

4. Consequently, benevolence agrees with the nature of God. (From 3.)
5. Now, whatever agrees with the nature of what "is in effect being in general" agrees with the nature of things.
6. Therefore, benevolence agrees with the nature of things. (From 1, 4, and 5.) (*TV* 621).

The third argument uses "agreement" in yet another sense. Edwards's point is roughly that the nature of things is divine benevolence. Human benevolence agrees with it because it is its image.

Edwards is an occasionalist like Malebranche, an idealist like Berkeley, and a mental phenomenalist like Hume. What are "vulgarly" called causal relations are mere constant conjunctions. *True* causes necessitate their effects. Because God's will alone meets this condition, God is the only true cause. He is also the only true substance. Physical objects are collections of "corporeal ideas" (ideas of color, for example, or solidity, resistance, and so on). Minds are series of "thoughts" or "perceptions." Any substance underlying perceptions, thoughts, and corporeal ideas would be something that "subsisted by itself, and stood underneath and kept up" physical and mental properties. But God alone subsists by Himself, stands underneath, and keeps up thoughts, perceptions, solidity, color, and other corporeal qualities (ideas). Hence, "the substance of bodies [and minds] at last becomes either nothing, or nothing but the Deity acting in that particular manner . . . where he thinks fit."[45] The only real cause and the only real substance are thus God Himself. God's essence, however, is love. The real nature of things, then, is an infinite and omnipotent benevolence.

Our benevolence "agrees with" this in the sense that it resembles it or is an image of it. The thrust of Edwards's argument is therefore this. Benevolence is appropriate because it mirrors reality. Nature's activity is really *God's* activity. (Because God is the only true substance and the only true cause, He is *natura naturans*.) Love is thus "natural" because it imitates the activity of "Nature" itself.

45. Jonathan Edwards, "Of Atoms" (*Scientific and Philosophical Writings*, p. 215). The quotations are from an argument "proving" that God is the only substance underlying corporeal properties. Edwards clearly thinks, however, that similar considerations show that God is also the only substance underlying mental qualities.

Edwards's theistic metaphysics is also implicit in his fourth argument.

> 1. Harmony among beings is more agreeable to the nature of things than disharmony.
> 2. Benevolence (the consent of being to being) promotes (or is) harmony among beings.
> 3. Therefore, benevolence agrees with the nature of things. (*TV* 100–101)

Edwards assumes that whatever promotes harmony in a system accords or agrees with its nature. This is plausible when the system is organic or social. In Edwards's opinion, being in general *is* an organic or social system. The only things that exist without qualification are minds, and minds form a social system in which God is sovereign.[46]

Benevolence, then, has a "foundation in the nature of things." Because the spiritual sense is an *expression* of benevolence, Edwards concludes that it, too, is founded "in the nature of things." "The idea we obtain by this spiritual sense" is thus "a knowledge or perception" of something outside our minds, a true "representation" of something "without," namely, God's moral perfection and excellence and its created reflections (*TV* 622f).

Edwards's defense of the objectivity of the new spiritual sense has four steps. (1) Benevolence agrees with the nature of things. The world is an interconnected system of minds and ideas in which the only true substance and cause are an infinite and omnipotent love. Human benevolence, therefore, is an appropriate or fitting response to reality. (2) A delight in benevolence also agrees with reality. Benevolence is pleased by benevolence; it relishes it, or delights in it, for its own sake (*TV* 546–49). If benevolence is an appropriate response to reality, so, too, then, is benevolence's delight in benevolence. (3) Delight in benevolence is identified with a perception of its spiritual beauty. (4) The redeemed's spiritual perceptions are veridical. Spiritual sensations are a "representation" of something

---

46. Edwards also thinks that God (who is "in effect being in general") is triune and thus inherently social.

"without," that is, they are noetic or perceptionlike. In Berkeley's words, they have "outness." The second step established that our spiritual sense is in order, that its motions are appropriate to reality. If spiritual sensations were merely subjective feelings such as indignation and admiration or physical pleasure and pain, then the second step would only show that these feelings are appropriate affective responses to their objects. But the third step informs us that spiritual sensations *are not* mere feelings; they are apparent cognitions. Because the apparent cognitions are an appropriate response to reality, they are a "knowledge or perception" of something "without"; the representations are "true representations."

How successful is Edwards's defense? The first two steps are plausible. Although Edwards's occasionalism, idealism, and mental phenomenalism undoubtedly strengthened his belief in benevolence's agreement with the nature of things, similar conclusions follow from any theistic (or at least Christian) metaphysics. The second step is also plausible. An essential feature of an appropriate response is itself appropriate. And Edwards's fourth step follows from his second and third.

The problem is the third step. Because Edwards's identification of spiritual perception with a kind of pleasure is suspect (see the first two subsections), his defense is not fully successful. Nevertheless, Edwards's reflections provide a promising start. Benevolence may really *be* spiritual perception's underlying mechanism. The nature of this perception, though, and its relation to benevolence, need further clarification.

The Appeal to Theistic Metaphysics and the Problem of Circularity

The most instructive feature of Edwards's defense is the way it uses theistic metaphysics. I suspect that any persuasive justification of a spiritual sense's reliability will do the same. Is it therefore circular? It is not *if* theistic metaphysics can be established without appealing to spiritual perceptions. Does Edwards think it can? He believes that theistic metaphysics is supported by natural reason and sometimes suggests that the rational evidence is sufficient. On the other hand, he also talks as if it often will not *seem* sufficient to those with unconverted hearts.

If Edwards is right, justifications of spiritual perceptions are not circular in the sense that they employ premises that explicitly or implicitly assert that spiritual perceptions are reliable. Nor are they circular in the sense that they employ premises that *in principle* can only be known to be true by those who rely on their spiritual sense. As we shall see in the following section, however, there is a de facto psychological or causal connection between having spiritual perceptions and appreciating the force of the evidence for a theistic metaphysics and thereby appreciating the force of justifications of the spiritual sense's reliability. It seems, then, both that these justifications are not logically or epistemically circular *and* that those who lack spiritual perceptions, or distrust them, will normally find them unpersuasive.

An example may clarify my point. Suppose that someone sees the force of an inductive argument for the guilt of his brother only after he has been persuaded of his brother's guilt. (Perhaps his brother confessed.) Is the argument circular? Is it circular for him? Not clearly. The nature of his noetic equipment is not such that he cannot know the premises without knowing the conclusion. Indeed, he may have firmly believed that the premises are true. Nor is its nature such that he *cannot* see that the premises establish the conclusion. The fault is not with his noetic equipment but with his attachment to his brother, which blinded him to the force of the evidence and prevented him from using his noetic equipment properly. The relation between believing the conclusion and recognizing the force of the argument for it is thus extrinsic or accidental. His inability to appreciate the weight of the evidence prior to accepting the argument's conclusion is the result of a psychological or moral aberration, not a matter of logic or a consequence of the nature of his cognitive faculties.

Edwards's view is similar. The reliability of our spiritual sense can be justified by a theistic metaphysics that is itself adequately supported by evidence accessible to natural reason. But sin blinds us to the evidence's force. There is thus a causal connection between spiritual perception and rational persuasion. Appeals to spiritual perceptions play no role, however, in the justificatory process itself. If this is correct, it seems misleading to say that the reliability of the spiritual sense cannot be justified without circularity. But this is a difficult issue, and we will return to it in Chapter 4.

The Bearing of Edwards's Theory
on Contemporary Discussions

Edwards's account of the sense of the heart goes some way toward filling an important gap in contemporary discussions—the failure adequately to explain *how* theistic belief-producing mechanisms operate. The issue is important for two reasons.

First, the nature of the mechanism has a bearing on its reliability. For example, Freud offers several accounts of the nature of the theistic belief-producing mechanism that, if true, cast doubt on its reliability. Theists can defuse criticisms of this sort by providing alternative and equally plausible accounts of the mechanism's operation that do not impugn its reliability.

The second reason is this. On reading the *Vedas*, an Advaitin may find himself spontaneously believing that they express the Nirguna Brahman. On reading the *Iśa Upanishad* or having a monistic mystical experience, he may find himself spontaneously believing that all differences are unreal or that the impersonal Brahman is ultimate. On surveying the evidence, he may conclude that Advaita Vedānta has fewer difficulties than its rivals and is therefore more likely to be true. If these beliefs are true, theism is false. On the face of it, the theist's beliefs and the Advaitin's beliefs are formed in similar ways. The same sort of belief-producing mechanism seems involved in both cases. If it is, then if one is reliable, so presumably is the other. And yet they cannot *both* be reliable, for they produce conflicting beliefs. Hence, neither seems reliable.

What is needed is an explanation of the difference between theistic and (for example) Advaitin or Mahāyānan belief-producing mechanisms, together with an indication of why the former are reliable and the latter are not.

Edwards may provide some assistance here for he has the beginnings of an account of how one theistic belief-producing mechanism operates. His account is also the *right* sort. If the mechanism is (a function of?) benevolence rather than wish fulfillment or the working out of an oedipal complex, there may be less reason for thinking it untrustworthy. Again, if (1) the disposition to form true religious beliefs is a function of benevolence or love, (2) benevolence or love agrees with the nature of things, and (3) the love of being in general is either absent or less fully developed in Advaita or Mahāyāna, one has some indication of why the theist's religious belief-producing mechanism is more reliable than the latter's.[47]

My point, of course, is not that Edwards *has* provided a fully adequate account but that some account is needed to defuse certain sorts of criticism and that the kind of account Edwards presents is the *right* kind.

These brief remarks are not sufficient to allay the spectres of subjectivism and relativism; those issues will be addressed in Chapters 4 and 5. Our task now is to look at Edwards's account of religious reasoning more closely.

Sanctified Reason

Edwards uses "reason" in two closely related senses. Sometimes the term refers to "ratiocination, or a power of inferring by arguments" (DSL 18). At others it refers to "the power . . . an intelligent being has to judge of the truth of propositions . . . immediately by only looking on the propositions" as well as to ratiocination (Misc. 1340,T 219).[48] The difference between these characterizations is not important; in

47. It will be more difficult for a Christian to cast aspersions on (e.g.) a Vaisnava's religious belief-producing mechanism. Vaisnavism is a theistic grace religion that values love. To discriminate between the Christian's and the Vaisnava's intuitions, one must either (1) distinguish between the quality of the Christian's and the Vaisnava's benevolence, or (2) appeal to cultural or (less plausibly) psychological or moral factors that impede the proper operations of the Vaisnava's spiritual faculties. The Christian might, however, concede that some true beauty *is* perceived in the *Bhagavad-Gītā* and the theistic Upanishads. For he or she may think that these texts, too, are revelations though not as perfect as the Christian revelation. Cf. Clement of Alexandria's claim that philosophy may have been "given to the Greeks directly; for it was a 'schoolmaster,' to bring Hellenism to Christ, as the Law was for the Hebrews" (Henry Bettenson, *The Early Christian Fathers* [London: Oxford University Press, 1963], p. 232).

48. In *Freedom of the Will* Edwards asserts that propositions are self-evident when they express necessary truths or things present to (immediately perceived by) the mind. Examples are mathematical propositions, analytic truths, metaphysical principles, true moral statements, and reports of present ideas and sensations (see pp. 153, 181–82, and 259).

either case, "reason's work is to perceive truth and not excellency" (DSL 18). Excellency and what pertains to it are perceived by the heart. Even though Edwards concedes that there is a more extended sense in which "reason" refers to "the faculty of mental perception in general" (DSL 18), he clearly prefers the stricter usage. His official view is that of other modern philosophers who deny that reason has an affective dimension (a love of the good, for example, or a delight in excellence).[49]

Grace affects reason as well as the heart. "Common grace" helps the faculties "to do that more fully which they do by nature," strengthening "the natural principles [e.g., conscience] against those things that tend to stupify [sic] it and to hinder its free exercise." "Special grace," on the other hand, "causes those things to be in the soul that are above nature; and causes them to be in the soul habitually" (Misc. 626, T 111). Special grace sanctifies by infusing benevolence or true virtue (viz., the love of being in general). Infused benevolence is the basis of a new epistemic principle; a sense of the heart that tastes, relishes, and perceives the beauty of holiness (i.e., benevolence). By its means, the sanctified acquire a new simple idea (the idea of "true beauty") that the unredeemed lack.[50] Because this idea is needed to understand divine matters properly, the "saints" are in a superior epistemic position. One cannot rightly understand God's moral attributes, for example, if one does not perceive their beauty. Nor can one adequately grasp truths that logically or epistemically depend on God's holiness and its splendor such as the infinite heinousness of sin or the appropriateness of God's aiming at His own glory. The saints also behold old data with new eyes. They perceive the stamp of divine splendor on the world's order and design, and on the events recorded in sacred history. They thereby acquire a more accurate sense of this evidence's force and impressiveness.

49. Although Edwards's identification with this tradition is not entirely straightforward. Edwards's sense of the heart, for example, is a *cognitive* faculty whereas (e.g.) Hutcheson's is not. Furthermore, even though Edwards normally assigns the sense of the heart to the will (i.e., to our affective nature), he sometimes assigns it to the understanding. See, for example, RA 206.

50. The saints are not wholly passive with respect to the reception of this new simple idea, for they can increase its clarity and intensity. They can do so, however, only "by the practice of virtue and holiness—for we cannot have the idea without the adapted disposition of mind" (Misc. 123, T 246).

The perception of spiritual beauty was discussed in the preceding section. This section focuses on another epistemic effect of special grace. The new principle that God infuses "sanctifies the reasoning faculty and assists it to see the clear evidence there is of the truth of religion in rational arguments, and that in two ways, viz., as it removes prejudices and so lays the mind more open to the force of arguments, and also secondly, as it positively enlightens and assists it to see the force of rational arguments . . . by adding greater light, clearness and strength to the judgment" (Misc. 628, T 251).[51] There is nothing intrinsically supernatural about many of these benefits. The *cause* of the mind's reasoning soundly is supernatural, but the effect (sound reasoning) need not be;[52] the spirit simply helps us use our natural epistemic faculties rightly.

What sorts of "prejudices" interfere with reason's "free exercise"? "Opinions arising from imagination" are one example. They "take us as soon as we are born, are beat into us by every act of sensation, and so grow up with us from our very births; and by that means grow into us so fast that it is almost impossible to root them out, being as it were so incorporated with our very minds that whatsoever is objected to them, contrary thereunto, is as if it were dissonant to the very constitution of them. Hence, men come to make what they can actually perceive by their senses, or immediate and outside reflection into their own souls, the standard of possibility and impossibility" (Prejudices 196). Biases arising from temperament, education, custom, and fashion furnish other examples (Mind 68 and Subjects 384 and 387).

Sin's essence is a failure to obey the love commandment. Those who do not love being in general love "private systems." Their loves are partial, extending to only some beings. They are also inordinate; lives are centered on the self or more extensive private systems rather than on God (who is "in effect" being in general) and the creatures who are absolutely dependent on Him and reflect His glory.[53]

---

51. Insofar as special grace simply strengthens natural principles, its effects are the same as those of common grace.

52. The exceptions will become clear as we proceed.

53. For a fuller treatment of these points, see my "Original Sin," in *Philosophy and the Christian Faith*, ed. Thomas V. Morris (Notre Dame, Ind.: University of Notre Dame Press, 1988).

Sin has noetic consequences. Edwards refers, for example, to "the great subjection of the soul in its fallen state to the external senses" (Misc. 782, T 122). (This subjection is presumably a consequence of the soul's inordinate love of temporal goods.)[54] Again, self-love blinds us to everything that does not bear on immediate self-interest (*OS* 145–57). In addition, "the mind of man is naturally full of enmity against the doctrines of the gospel" that cause "arguments that prove their truth . . . to lose their force upon the mind" (*RA* 307). (God crosses our self-love and love of temporal things, and this arouses hostility.)[55]

Our corrupt inclinations even affect our sense of what is and is not reasonable. "Common inclination or the common dictates of inclination, are often called common sense." A person who says that the doctrine of eternal damnation offends common sense is using the expression in this way. But the inclinations behind this judgment have been shaped by an insensibility to "the great evil of sin." They are therefore corrupt (Misc. Obs. 253).

William James has suggested that our judgments of credibility reflect what we have a use for, what vitally concerns us. "In . . . the sense in which we contrast reality with simple *un*reality, and in which one thing is said to have *more* reality than another, and to be more believed, reality means simply relation to our emotional and active life. This is the only sense that the word ever has in the mouths of practical men. In this sense whatever excites and stimulates our interests is real."[56] "The natural propensity of man is to believe that whatever has great value for life is thereby certified as true."[57] Our judgments of truth and reality, in other words, are (partly) functions of our emotional engagement. Edwards would agree. If our interests are badly misdirected, our

54. Cf. Plato in *Phaedo* and elsewhere. As noted, there is an important Platonic strand in Puritanism.

55. "Hostility" may be too strong. But we do have a natural tendency to *resist* demands that cross our self-love and love of temporal goods by diverting our attention to other things, for example, or by rationalizing.

56. William James, *The Principles of Psychology*, vol. 2 (Cambridge: Harvard University Press, 1981), p. 924 (James's emphases).

57. William James, *The Varieties of Religious Experience* (New York: Modern Library, c. 1902), p. 500, n.

judgments of what is and is not credible will be correspondingly distorted.

Grace frees the mind from these "prejudices." An unprejudiced reason, however, is not dispassionate. For it is affected by *epistemically benign* feelings and inclinations. A love of wider systems alone checks self-interest. Nor is it sufficient to replace hostility toward religion with indifference or neutrality; the heart must be receptive to it. An unprejudiced reason is also affected by natural motions of the heart as well as by true benevolence (gratitude for one's being, for example, or a sense that it would be unfitting for the injustice that evades human tribunals to escape punishment).[58] And because our love of temporal goods is not subordinate to a love of eternity, it is inordinate, and the latter is needed to correct it.[59]

Another point is relevant as well. Natural reason reveals many truths about God and our relation to Him. Yet even at the level of nature these truths are not properly understood if the heart lacks a due sense of the natural good and evil in them[60] (a proper sense of the natural unfittingness of disobeying the world's sovereign, for example, a horror of the natural evils consequent on offenses against Him, or a proper sense of the natural benefits He has bestowed on us and of the obligations these gifts create).

I conclude, then, that *common* grace not only inhibits the action of passional factors corrupting reason; it also causes better natural affections to influence it (at least temporarily). *Sanctifying* grace replaces the effects of corrupt affections by the influences of true benevolence. A reason that is exercising itself "freely" and without "prejudice," therefore, is affected by passional factors.

But grace does more than remove the impediments ("prejudices") hindering reason's free exercise by restructuring our affections. It

---

58. See Miscellany 353 (T 110–11) for an instance in which a natural sentiment legitimately affects the reasoning process. Our sense of justice (rightly) leads us to suppose that the world is governed by it.

59. This need not involve an infusion of supernatural principles. A love of God for His holiness is saving and truly supernatural. A love of God based on disinterested admiration of His greatness and on gratitude for His temporal benefits is not.

60. Natural goods and evils are those that can be appreciated without the help of infused supernatural principles (i.e., without a love of being in general and the sense of divine beauty that is rooted in it).

adds "greater light, clearness and strength to the judgment." Edwards refers us to Miscellany 408 for "one way" in which it does so.[61] That entry argues that ideas of spiritual things "appear more lively and with greater strength and impression" after conversion and that, consequently, "their circumstances and various relations and connections between themselves and with other ideas appear more" (Misc. 408, T 249–50).

How does the spirit accomplish this? By focusing the mind's attention on "actual ideas." Thought has a tendency to substitute signs for ideas, to use signs without having the "actual" (i.e., lively, clear, and distinct) ideas they signify. The signs may be words or (confused) ideas of "some sensible part, . . . effect, . . . or concomitant, or a few sensible circumstances" of what we are thinking about (Misc. 782, T 116).[62] Our ability to make this substitution is advantageous because some actual ideas are not easy to elicit and because thought would be too slow without it; it serves us well for "many of the common purposes of thinking." Nevertheless, it is a *dis*advantage when "we are at a loss concerning a connection or consequence, or have a new inference to draw, or would see the force of some new argument," for the "use of signs . . . causes mankind to run into a multitude of errors" (Misc. 782, T 117–18). The tendency to make this substitution is strongest when the ideas terms signify are ideas of "kinds and sorts," or things "of a spiritual nature, or things that consist in the ideas, acts, and exercises of minds" (Misc. 782, T 115). This tendency infects *all* (and not merely religious) thinking and can be remedied by attending to ideas instead of the signs that express them.[63]

Actual ideas and attention are closely connected. An idea will not become actual unless one "dwells" on it; "attentive reflection" is necessary. Indeed, "attention of the mind" itself consists "very much" in "exciting the actual idea and making it as lively and clear as we can"

61. There is no indication of what other "ways" Edwards had in mind—if any.
62. Why must the parts, effects, and so on be sensible? Presumably, because sensible ideas are easier to excite and because sensible things are the kind "we are mainly concerned with" in ordinary life (T 177).
63. Cf. Locke's chapters on the imperfection and abuse of words (*HU* 3.9–11). In 11.8–9, Locke tells us to avoid terms that do not stand for clear and distinct, or determinate, ideas.

(Misc. 782, T 118). But attention is difficult. Even in temporal affairs, taking an "ideal view" (having actual ideas) often depends "not merely on the force of our thoughts but the circumstances we are in, or some special accidental situation and concurrence of things in the course of our thoughts and meditations, or some particular incident in providence that excites a sense of things" (ibid. 121–22). As for *eternal* matters, our attention is distracted by "the great subjection of the soul . . . to the external senses" and by "the direction of the inclinations . . . [away] from . . . things as they are" (ibid. 122). Grace remedies this defect, for one of its effects is to "engage the attention of the mind, with more fixedness and intenseness to that kind of objects; which causes it to have a clearer view of them" (DSL 9–10). Grace "makes even the speculative notions more lively" by assisting and engaging "the attention of the mind" (*RA* 307). Yet why should such extraordinary measures be necessary?

Actual ideas of kinds or sorts are clear and distinct ideas "of those things that are principally essential" in the idea, those things wherein it "most essentially consists" (Misc. 782, T 113, 114). Edwards is undoubtedly thinking of Locke's theory of ideas. Our ideas of God, human nature, and perplexity (Edwards's examples) are complex. The idea of God, for instance, is constructed from the ideas of "supremacy, of supreme power, of supreme government, of supreme knowledge, of will, etc;" (Ibid. 113). Actual ideas of complex ideas such as these involve actual ideas of the ("principally essential"?) simple ideas that compose them.

Actual ideas of things pertaining to good or evil present another difficulty. One cannot have them without being suitably affected, pleased or displeased as the case may be. Actual ideas of these things involve the heart.

Finally, actual ideas of "the ideas, acts, and exercises of minds" are "repetitions of those very things." One cannot have them without experiencing what they are ideas of (Misc. 238, T 247).[64] (Actual

---

64. Although Edwards overstates his case, there is a measure of truth in it. The idea of an idea is not another instance of it but does include it. The ideas of fear and love are not fear and love, but an experience of these emotions may be needed to acquire them or to have the same ideas of fear and love that others do. Perhaps, too, ideas of this sort only become lively and vivid when we recall the relevant experiences, that is, when how they "feel" comes back to us.

ideas of the will or inclination, or the affections, and of things pertaining to them, will thus also involve the heart. An idea of love, for example, is a repetition of it, and love's seat is the heart.)

Our failure to attend to actual ideas has two causes. Sometimes we substitute words and images for ideas we have. Sometimes we lack relevant simple ideas. Both can adversely affect religious reasoning. Those parts of the idea of God that everyone has (ideas of His power, knowledge, and justice, for instance) are not attended to or, when they are, do not affect us with a proper sense of the natural good or evil associated with them. Other parts are simply missing. Without the simple idea of true beauty, people cannot understand God's holiness and the facts that depend on it such as the infinite heinousness of sin or the infinite importance of holiness. Nor can the "carnal" understand genuine benevolence and other properties and qualifications which the elect share with God. Because the idea of true benevolence is a repetition of it, the truly benevolent alone have an actual idea of it. Those who are not benevolent only discern its circumstances, effects, and so on, "explaining" the idea of benevolence to themselves and others in "general terms" that do not adequately delimit it (Misc. 123, T 245f).[65]

It should by now be clear how sin affects reasoning. Our immersion in temporal concerns distracts us so that we do not attend to our ideas. Our subjection to the senses aggravates the tendency to substitute words and other sensible signs for ideas, and our disordered loves make it difficult for us to appreciate even natural goods and evils associated with religion. (For example, our blunted conscience blinds us to the natural fittingness of obeying God's commands, and our inordinate attachment to the present life leads us to neglect more im-

___

65. Although "apprehension" or "an ideal view or contemplation of the thing thought of" (i.e., having an actual idea of it) are closely connected with a sense of the heart, they are not identical with it. The former is contrasted with "mere cogitation," "which is a kind of mental reading wherein we don't look on the things themselves but only on those signs of them that are before our eyes." The latter is contrasted with "mere speculation or understanding of the head," which includes "all that understanding that is without any proper ideal apprehension or view" and all understanding that does not "consist in or imply some motion of the will," that is, that does not involve the heart (Misc. 782, T 118–19). These distinctions cut across each other. A sense of the heart is not needed to "apprehend" (take "an ideal view" of) mathematical objects.

portant natural goods that extend beyond it.) A lack of true benevolence (which is sin's essence) makes it impossible to understand God's holiness (which consists in it) or to appreciate its beauty.

We are now also in a position to understand why rational arguments for religious truths are not always convincing. Miscellanies 201 (T 246–47) and 408 (T 249–50) imply that a conviction of reality is created by (1) an idea's clarity and liveliness, (2) its internal coherence and coherence with our other ideas, and (3) its agreement with "the nature and constitution of our minds themselves." Why, then, do religious ideas so often fail to carry conviction? Partly because the clarity and intensity of spiritual ideas is a function of "the practice of virtue and holiness" (Misc. 123, T 246) and our own practice falls woefully short, and partly because the "tempers" or "frames" of the ungodly are not suited to them. (See William James's claim that what seems true and real to us is what we have use for.) It is possible that those without spiritual frames cannot even discern their coherence. Sang Hyun Lee argues that because beauty, on Edwards's view, consists in harmony or proportion, a perception of beauty is a perception of harmony.[66] If proportion and pleasing order are included in coherence, unaided reason may have difficulty grasping it; for it may miss the "sweet harmony" among the ideas of religion and between those ideas and other ideas. (Consider those who reject religion because it does not seem to "fit" or "hang together" with science, although they concede there is no formal inconsistency.)

Special or sanctifying grace remedies these defects by enabling us to attend more easily to the actual ideas the words of religion stand for and by disposing the heart to be suitably affected by the natural and supernatural good and evil associated with them. Common grace has similar effects, but (because it does not replace the love of private systems with true benevolence) it does not furnish the mind

---

66. Sang Hyun Lee, *The Philosophical Theology of Jonathan Edwards* (Princeton: Princeton University Press, 1988). Whether this interpretation is compatible with the simplicity of the idea of true beauty is a moot point. On my account (second section), the idea of true beauty is ontologically distinct from the order or harmony that underlies the disposition to excite it in suitably disposed subjects.

with actual ideas of true virtue and true beauty and only affects it with a sense of the relevant *natural* goods and evils.

The sense of divine beauty alone is intrinsically supernatural. A reason that has been freed from the bonds of imagination, prejudice, and narrow self-interest, attends to ideas of God's being, power, knowledge, justice, munificence, and other "natural" attributes and is suitably affected by the natural good and evil associated with them is not functioning above its nature.[67] A reason that has been strengthened in these ways is capable, however, of seeing the force of rational arguments for the truths of "natural religion" (i.e., for truths about God that depend neither logically nor epistemically on the ideas of holiness and true beauty). A suitably disposed natural reason is thus capable of establishing God's existence and general nature, and some of our obligations toward Him. Truths that depend on the ideas of holiness and true beauty can also be established by rational arguments, but the force of these can only be appreciated by people with spiritual frames.

Edwards and Evidentialism

Edwards was the philosophical heir of rationalists and empiricists whose confidence in reason was comparatively unqualified. He was the theological heir of a Reformed tradition that distrusted humanity's natural capacities. Did he succeed in coherently weaving these apparently inconsistent strands together? The answer, I believe, is a qualified "Yes."

The key is a distinction between good rational arguments and the conditions necessary for their acceptance. I may have a good argument against smoking, for example, but my desire to smoke prevents me from appreciating its force. What is needed is not a better argument but a reorientation of my desires.

---

67. Although, if I understand Edwards correctly, our bondage to the senses and self-interest can be fully eliminated only by God's infusing true virtue, that is, by His infusing a supernatural principle. Without a supernatural principle to govern them, our natural principles fall into disorder. "Man's nature, being left to itself, forsaken of the spirit of God . . . of itself became exceedingly corrupt" (*OS* 279). "The absence of positive good principles [holiness or true virtue] . . . leaving the common natural principles of self-love, natural appetite, etc. (which were in man in innocence) . . . will certainly be followed with corruption" (*OS* 381).

Edwards's position is roughly this. Although reason is capable of generating good rational arguments for God's existence, His providential government of human affairs, predestination, and many other theological and metaphysical doctrines, self-deception, prejudice, self-interest, and other passional factors make it difficult for us to see their force. These faults cannot be corrected by applying Descartes's rules for correct thinking, Locke's "measures . . . to regulate our assent and moderate our persuasion,"[68] or other methods of this sort. What is needed is a set of excellences that are themselves expressions of morally desirable character traits and rightly ordered affections. The defects distorting human reasoning are deeply rooted in human nature and can only be eliminated by the appropriate virtues.

Two features of Edwards's position are especially significant. First, the epistemic virtues are not merely negative; they involve more than the exclusion of the passions and selfish partialities that subvert reason. Nor are the epistemic virtues confined to noncontroversial excellences such as the love of truth. They include properly ordered natural affections such as gratitude and a love of being in general that God infuses into the hearts of His elect. These affections not only cast out others that adversely affect reasoning; they also affect it themselves. Under their influence, we reason differently and more accurately.

The other significant feature is this. Two views should be distinguished. One is that there are circumstances in which it is legitimate for people's passions and affections to make up deficiencies in the evidence. Although the (objective) evidence is not sufficient to warrant belief, one is entitled to let one's passional nature tip the balance. The other is that a person's passional nature is sometimes needed to evaluate the evidence properly (to assess its force accurately). The first view is often attributed to James. Edwards holds the second.

Edwards's position differs significantly from the more familiar views of James, Kierkegaard, and others who appeal to passional factors. Edwards is a foundationalist and an evidentialist. A proper, and therefore rational, belief must be self-evident or based on adequate

68. *HU,* "Introduction," section 3.

evidence. A properly held belief *in God* rests on evidence (the beauty of scripture, the effects of the Holy Spirit in our souls, apparent design, and so on).[69] But unlike most evidentialists, Edwards believes that passional factors are needed to appreciate the evidence's *force*. Only those with properly disposed hearts can read the evidence rightly.

Edwards's view thus also differs from Locke's. Fully rational judgments are not only determined by one's evidence and evidential standards; they are also determined by feelings and attitudes that express theological virtues.

But are not the promptings of true benevolence *themselves* evidence of a sort? And if so, is not the difference between Edwards and Locke illusory? I suggest that it is not.

The promptings of true benevolence in this context just *are* the assessments of the force of a body of evidence, *e,* made by a truly benevolent heart.[70] Suppose that one treats this assessment as a new piece of evidence, e^1. If one does, one must now assess *its* force (or the force of one's other evidence plus e^1). But this new assessment also reflects the state of one's heart. It, too, therefore, must be treated as a new piece of evidence, e^2, whose force (or the combined force of $e + e^1 + e^2$) must in turn be assessed. Hence, if one's assessment of the force of a body of evidence is itself part of one's evidence, then either the force of some of one's evidence is not assessed or one's evidence includes an infinite number of items.

Treating true benevolence's assessment of the force of the evidence as a piece of evidence is as misguided as treating an intellectually honest, critical, and fairminded historian's assessment of the strength of her argument as one of her premises. One's evidence must be distinguished from one's take on it.

It does not follow that true benevolence's take on the evidence is a "nonrational ground of belief" in Richard Swinburne's sense. A nonrational ground for belief that *p* is a reason for "believing it to be true

69. One must remember, however, that the most compelling evidence is the divine beauty or splendor that the elect see in the Gospel, in Christ, in the saints, and so on. (The belief that these are truly beautiful is properly basic.)

70. The assessments made by a truly benevolent heart must be distinguished from its perception of true beauty. The latter *is* a new piece of evidence.

other than that it [is] likely to be true." It might be good, for instance, to hold a certain belief although the evidence seems to count against it. (For example, respect for persons might entail a duty to think well of them in spite of appearances.) Or it might be prudentially worthwhile to hold a belief. But (Swinburne argues) even if you have a nonrational ground for believing *p*, you cannot believe *p* unless you believe that your evidence makes *p* probable. To get yourself to believe *p*, you must therefore get yourself to believe that your evidence supports *p*. Yet "to get yourself to believe that your evidence makes *p* probable" when it (now) seems to you that it does not involves "getting yourself to change your inductive standards by adopting standards which you now believe to be incorrect, or by getting yourself to forget about some of the unfavorable evidence, or by getting yourself to acquire new favorable evidence through looking only where favorable evidence is to be found and then forgetting the selective character of your investigation." It thus involves deliberately inducing beliefs that are irrational by your present standards.[71]

True benevolence's assessment of the evidence is not a nonrational ground for belief in this sense. It does not lead the saints to construct new inductive or deductive standards, forget about some of the evidence, or engage in selective investigation. Nor does it provide them with a *reason* for doing so. True benevolence is not a nonrational ground for belief in Swinburne's sense because it is not a *ground* for belief at all, although its presence *does* partially explain why the saints hold the beliefs they do. In the same way, a good scientist's impartiality, intellectual honesty, and desire for the truth help explain why she holds the beliefs she does and not the views of some less scrupulous or more credulous colleague. But they are not *grounds* for her belief.

The position Edwards represents must be distinguished, then, from other more familiar views. Whether it can be defended against charges of subjectivism, circularity, and relativism will be discussed in Chapters 4 and 5.

---

71. Although they will not *seem* irrational once you have acquired them, and although (after you have acquired them) they will be rationally held in the sense that they follow from the evidence you will then have by the inductive standards you will then hold. (For Swinburne's discussion, see *Faith and Reason* [Oxford: Clarendon, 1981], pp. 82–92.)

Before turning to these issues, however, it will be helpful to examine John Henry Newman and William James. For they believe
that the suspect features of religious reasoning also characterize informal reasoning in other areas. Those who indict religious reasoning for displaying these features may find themselves forced to
choose between wholesale dismissal of argumentation whose credentials are not in serious question and a selective and therefore inconsistent application of their own epistemic standards.

2

John Henry Newman and
the "Grammar of Assent"

Consider these chains of reasoning. (1) Our conviction that Great Britain is an island is well-founded. We have no doubt that it is true. But if asked to give our evidence for it, we can only respond that "first, we have been so taught in our childhood, and it is so on all the maps; next, we have never heard it contradicted or questioned; on the contrary, everyone whom we have heard speak on the subject of Great Britain, every book we have read, invariably took it for granted; our whole national history, the routine transactions and current events of the country, our social and commercial system, our political relations with foreigners, imply it in one way or another. Numberless facts, or what we consider facts, rest on the truth of it; no received fact rests on its being otherwise" (GA 234–35).[1] Our belief that Britain is an island is not based on a rigorous deductive or

---

1. John Henry Newman, *An Essay in Aid of a Grammar of Assent* (London 1870; reprint, Notre Dame, Ind.: University of Notre Dame Press, 1979), hereafter *GA*. Relevant discussions can also be found in several of Newman's other works: *The Theological Papers of John Henry Newman on Faith and Certainty*, ed. Hugo M. de Achaval and J. Derek Holmes (Oxford: Clarendon, 1976), hereafter *TP*; "Faith and Reason, Contrasted as Habits of Mind," "The Nature of Faith in Relation to Reason," and "Love the Safeguard of Faith against Superstition," in *Fifteen Sermons Preached before the University of Oxford* (Oxford, 1843; reprint, Westminster, Md.: Christian Classics, 1966), hereafter FRC, FR, and LSF, respectively; and "Faith without Sight," in *Parochial Sermons*, vol. 2 (London 1834–42; reprint, London: J. G. F. & J. Rivington, 1844), hereafter FWS.

inductive argument. But it *is* reasonable; a variety of independent considerations support it and nothing supports its denial.

(2) A historian of the Middle Ages asserts that the *Aeneid* could not be a thirteenth-century forgery. Her conviction is partly based on her knowledge of the capacities of the medieval mind. This knowledge depends on a lifetime of reading and study. Although many of the considerations that contributed to it have been forgotten and others have merged into a general impression of what the medieval mind could and could not do, her knowledge is real. "We do not pretend to be able to draw the line between what the medieval intellect could and could not do; but we feel sure that at least it could not write the classics. An instinctive sense of this [as well as a faith in testimony] are the sufficient, but the undeveloped argument on which to ground our certitude" (*GA* 237).

(3) Just as we "instinctively" infer "the fact of a multiform and vast world, material and mental" from the "phenomena of sense," and just as a child instinctively recognizes in the "smiles or the frowns" of a face "not only a being external to himself but one whose looks elicit in him confidence or fear," so we spontaneously infer God's existence from "particular acts of conscience" (*GA* 67–68; see also 97, 102). Our experience of guilt and moral inadequacy "instinctively" suggests the presence of a "moral governor" and "judge."

(4) Someone argues: "The Catholic religion is true, because its objects, as present to my mind, control and influence my conduct as nothing else does." Or, it is true "because it has about it an odour of truth and sanctity . . . as perceptible to my moral nature as flowers to my sense, such as can only come from heaven." Or it is true "because it has never been to me anything but peace, joy, consolation and strength, all through my troubled life" (*GA* 174).

(5) " 'I think,' says the poor dying factory girl in the tale [Elizabeth Gaskell's *North and South*], 'if this should be the end of all, and if all I have been born for is just to work my heart and life away, and to sicken in this dree place, with those millstones in my ears forever, until I could scream out for them to stop and let me have a little piece of quiet, and with the fluff filling my lungs, until I thirst to death for one long deep breath of the clear air, and my mother gone, and I never able to tell her again how I loved her, and of all my trou-

bles—I think, if this life is the end, and that there is no God to wipe away all tears from all eyes, I could go mad!' Here," says Newman, "is an argument for the immortality of the soul" (*GA* 247).

None of these arguments meet rigorous deductive or inductive standards. Newman nonetheless believes that each is a *good* argument and that its conclusion is reasonable. This assessment rests on three convictions. (1) Many good arguments are neither deductively valid nor inductively sound. Their conclusions are not entailed by their premises. Nor can they be derived from them by inductive extrapolation (by generalizing from the character of a fair sample, for example, or by inferring that an event will occur because similar events have occurred under similar conditions in the past). They are, instead, inferences to the best explanation. A hypothesis is adopted because it provides a more plausible explanation of a range of facts than its competitors. The most plausible explanation of the facts cited in the first argument, for instance, is that Great Britain *is* an island.[2] (2) There is no "common measure between mind and mind" that can be used to conclusively settle disagreements (*GA* 82); on the contrary, reason is "personal" and reflects the experience and cast of mind of the person who employs it. The evidence is often too complicated and "delicate" to be fully articulated. (The second argument is a case in point.) Some evidence is only accessible to men and women who have immersed themselves in the subject matter or are extensively acquainted with the phenomenon under investigation. (A person whose conscience is deadened will not appreciate the third argument.) The evidence on which we rightly rely, then, is not always fully stateable or universally accessible and, so, cannot be used to secure general agreement. Even when the evidence *is* stateable and accessible, differences may remain. Although there are rules and guidelines for assessing informal reasoning, their application requires judgment. But judgments reflect the characters and biographies of the people who make them, and these vary from one person to an-

2. Many, if not most, of the sample arguments in the *Grammar of Assent* are inferences to the best explanation. Whether they all are is doubtful. The factory girl's argument, for example, does not clearly fit this pattern. (Although one *could* argue that the conviction that there is a God to wipe away all tears from all eyes represents her attempt to make the most sense of the factors of her unfortunate life.).

other. (3) Our hopes and fears, needs and desires, longings, "in-stincts," and "divinations" sometimes rightly affect our assessment of a body of evidence. The fourth and fifth arguments are examples.

Newman's pioneering recognition of the importance and ubiquity of inferences to the best explanation is no longer controversial. His other two contentions are. We will examine them in the following sections.

The Illative Sense

Newman calls the faculty of informal reasoning "the illative sense." "Illative" was "defined in contemporary dictionaries [from 1864 and 1901] in terms of 'inference; deduction; conclusion.' Newman may have noticed the word in Locke who writes of 'illation' as the intel-lectual faculty which 'consists in nothing but the perception of the connexion there is between the ideas, in each step of the deduction.' . . . The phrase 'illative conjuctions' is found in Whately's *Logic* in a passage which Newman helped to compose."[3] Newman's own usage is ambiguous. M. Jamie Ferreira points out that "the illative sense" sometimes refers to the power of "judging and concluding" in *all* its forms including those which are "biased and degraded" and that it sometimes refers to the power "in its perfection."[4]

The faculty is principally employed in three ways: (1) in conduct-ing an argument, (2) in assessing prior probabilities, and (3) in evalu-ating an argument's overall force.

In conducting an argument, the illative sense is used to "scruti-nize, sort, and combine" premises and to "correctly [employ] principles of whatever kind, facts or doctrines, experiences or tes-timonies, true or probable" (*GA* 282). Consider a dispute between two historians. Each has first to decide which "opinions . . . to put aside as nugatory," what evidence is relevant, what has "prima facie authority," and the relative weights to be placed on various kinds of evidence" ("tradition, analogy [with familiar historical phenomena?], isolated monuments and records, ruins, vague re-

3. David A. Pailin, *The Way to Faith* (London: Epworth Press, 1969), p. 144.
4. M. Jamie Ferreira, *Doubt and Religious Commitment* (Oxford: Clarendon, 1980), p. 35.

ports, legends . . . language," etc.). "Then arguments have to be balanced against each other." Finally, each must decide whether a conclusion can be drawn and how certain it is. "It is plain how incessant will be the call . . . for the exercise of judgment" (*GA* 284).

The illative sense, then, decides which considerations are relevant, assigns weights to different kinds of considerations, marshals the evidence in some sort of order, applies appropriate principles (those used in assessing testimony, for example), and balances the positive and negative considerations against each other. Although these things can be done well or badly, "it is plain . . . how little that judgment will be helped on by logic and how intimately it will be dependent upon the intellectual complexion of the" reasoner (*GA* 284). In causal inquiries, for example, judgments of relevance will be affected by whether "we view a subject" as a system of efficient causes or as a system of final causes (*GA* 290). Again, Gibbon's account of "the rise of Christianity is the mere subjective view of one who could not enter into its depth and power" (*GA* 291); by restricting his attention to surface phenomena, Gibbon failed to consider relevant facts and experiences.

Our illative sense is also responsible for judgments of antecedent probability. We legitimately dismiss some hypotheses and opinions without argument.[5] Those we cannot dismiss as irrelevant or absurd are assigned a certain probability. But these assignments "will vary . . . according to the particular intellect" that makes the assessments (*GA* 233). And we not only assign conflicting probabilities to the premises. Each of us also has "his own view concerning" the likelihood of the conclusion "prior to the evidence; this view will result from the character of his mind. . . . If he is indisposed to believe he will explain away very strong evidence; if he is disposed, he will accept very weak evidence" (LSF 226).

For example, one historian finds the proposition "No testimony should be received, except such as comes from competent witnesses"

5. "Unless we had the right . . . of ruling that propositions were irrelevant or absurd, I do not see how we could conduct an argument at all; our way would . . . be blocked up by extravagant principles and theories, gratuitous hypotheses, . . . unsupported statements, and incredible facts" (*GA* 293).

more plausible than "Tradition, though unauthenticated, being . . . in possession, has a prescription in its favor." Another does not. As a result, the historians assign different initial probabilities to the same events (*GA* 294). Again, Pascal's cumulative case argument for Christianity depends "upon the assumption that the facts of Christianity are beyond human nature" and that it is thus antecedently unlikely that human beings would have invented them. Hence, "as the powers of nature are placed at a high or low standard," the force of his argument "will be greater or less; and that standard will vary according to the respective dispositions, opinions, and experiences, of those to whom the argument is addressed" (*GA* 245). In short, before drawing a conclusion we assign degrees of probability (plausibility) to the argument's "antecedents" (principles, facts, testimony, and so on).[6] We also approach the argument with views of the conclusion's antecedent probability. These judgments reflect our experience, knowledge, and temperament and affect our evaluation of the argument's strength.

One of the illative sense's most important functions is to assess an argument's overall force. "The mind itself is more versatile and vigorous than any of its works, of which language [i.e., logic] is one, and it is only under its penetrating and subtle action that the margin disappears . . . between verbal argumentation and conclusions in the concrete. It determines what science cannot determine, the limit of converging probabilities and the reasons sufficient for a proof" (*GA* 281–82). It determines, that is, how *strongly* the argument's "antecedents" support its conclusion.[7] Assessments of an argument's force, too, reflect the histories and tempers of the persons who make them. For when it comes to "the question, what is to become of the

6. This is not the same as assigning weights. A fact we regard as certain and relevant may be given little weight.

7. Although the line between estimating antecedent probabilities, viewing the evidence from the perspective of certain assumptions, and so on, and assessing the argument's force is not sharp, they are in principle distinct. One's assessment of an argument's overall force is a *function* of one's assessment of prior probabilities, the assumptions with which one approaches the evidence, one's judgments of relevance, one's assessment of the degree to which the premises support the conclusion if true (i.e., of how probable they make it), and so on. It is not, however, just the *sum* of these things.

evidence, being what it is," each must decide "according to (what is called) the state of his heart" (LSF 227).

Just as there are no formal rules for producing or recognizing good poetry, so there are no formal rules for determining the truth in concrete matters. In "concrete reasonings," the "ultimate test of truth or error in our inferences" is "the trustworthiness of the Illative Sense that gives them its sanction" (GA 281). The ultimate test, in other words, is our own best judgment. My judgment, however, is irredeemably personal, for I can only view the various pieces of evidence "in the medium of *my* primary mental experiences, under the aspects which they spontaneously present to *me*, and with the aid of *my* best illative sense" (GA 318, my emphasis).

Formal reasoning (whether deductive or inductive) is not a real alternative to illative inference. The mind's acts of concrete reasoning are too subtle, varied, and intricate to be fully verbalized. Try, for example, to articulate the mental acts involved in arriving at the conclusion that the emendations of an early commentator on Shakespeare's *Henry V* are reliable (GA 217–22), or to adequately verbalize the grounds of one's impression that whatever the medieval mind could do, it could not produce the *Aeneid* (GA 235–37), or the "delicate and at first invisible touches" in an anonymous publication which point toward a certain author (GA 259). Because our reasoning cannot be fully symbolized, formal principles cannot get a firm grip on it.[8]

But (and this is the more important point) even if our concrete reasonings *could* be adequately symbolized, our illative sense would remain indispensable. Formal inference and concrete reasoning are not real alternatives since the former is an abstraction from the latter. Concrete reasoning is formal reasoning "carried out into the realities of life, its premises[9] being instinct with the substance and the momentum of the mass of probabilities, which acting upon each other in correction and confirmation, carry it home to the individual case" (GA 232–33). One employs illation in deploying formal arguments, for one's assessment of the premises' plausibility and of the relevance of the argument's conclusion to the case at hand rest on as-

---

8. Or, more accurately, they can only get a firm grip on the inadequate verbal (symbolic) representations that act as surrogates for our concrete reasonings.

9. Those schematized in the formal argument that is an abstraction from it?

sumptions and tacit understandings that cannot be reduced to formal principles.

"No Common Measure"

Their illative senses often lead people to opposed conclusions. Why is this the case? Partly because the "first principles . . . with which we start in reasoning on any given subject matter" are "very numerous and vary . . . with the persons who reason . . . only a few of them [being] received universally" (GA 66). Some historians, as we have seen, assume that "no testimony should be received, except such as comes from competent witnesses." Others assume that "tradition, though unauthenticated, being . . . in possession, has a prescription in its favour" (GA 294). Their assessments of evidence will correspondingly differ. Bishop Butler denied that "a revelation, which is to be received as true, ought to be written on the sun." Newman, on the other hand, thinks that "something may be said in [the claim's] favour" (GA 295). One's attitude toward it will obviously affect one's assessment of the evidence for an alleged revelation. Again, judgments of relevance are affected by the aspects under which a person views a subject—whether or not she looks on nature as a system of efficient rather than final causes, for example, or views thought as a language, or deliberation as a system of weights and balances. " 'Tacit understandings' " and "vague and impalpable notions of 'reasonableness' . . . make conclusions possible." But they are also "the pledge of their being contradictory. The conclusions vary with the particular writer, for each writes from his own point of view and with his own principles, and these admit of no common measure" (GA 287).[10]

Why do our first principles and points of view differ? The "intuitions, first principles, axioms, dictates of common sense, presumptions, presentiments, prepossessions, or prejudices" with which we approach a body of evidence are reflections of our experiences (TP 108). Because the latter vary, so will the former.

---

10. The point is not that these principles and points of view are not subject to argument, for they are. Supporting arguments, however, must themselves be assessed by the illative sense, and this assessment, too, will reflect "tacit understandings," "vague . . . notions of 'reasonableness'," and so on.

Our impression of an argument's overall force is also affected by "personal" factors. People sometimes withhold assent from an argument through "a vague feeling that a fault lay at" its "ultimate basis" or because of "some misgiving that the subject matter . . . was beyond the reach of the human mind." Again "moral causes, arising out of our condition, age, fortune," and so on, "prejudice," or lack of sustained attention can cause us to withhold assent. Or we may remain unpersuaded because "we throw the full *onus probandi* on the side of the conclusion," refusing to assent until the arguments are not merely good but conclusive (*GA* 142–44). These attitudes and vague convictions are rooted in our characters and personal histories. Because these differ, so too will our estimates of an argument's force.[11]

Assessments of an argument's force are also a function of our real or notional assents.[12] Newman's discussion of real assent is somewhat confusing. Real assents are assents to propositions that are really apprehended. Newman's distinction between notional and real apprehension, however, conflates the distinction between the apprehension of general and of singular propositions, and the distinction between "two modes of apprehending propositions," "as counters to be combined and calculated *inter se*" and "as signs to be 'cashed' in terms of their appropriate mental images" and associations.[13] The latter, though, is most important. Real apprehensions are "thingish and imaginative."[14]

One's assent to the force of an argument may depend on whether one's assent to its premises is real or not. For example, the argument from evil will not unduly trouble those whose assent to "Evil exists"

11. Although this is not Newman's point in these passages; at this juncture, he is trying to show that assent and inference are different mental acts.

12. Newman nowhere clearly makes this point, but I feel confident that he would endorse it.

13. John Hick, *Faith and Knowledge* (Ithaca: Cornell University Press, 1957), pp. 87–88.

14. H. H. Price, *Belief* (London: Allen & Unwin, 1969), p. 330. One really apprehends a proposition by dwelling on instances. "What matters," in these cases, "is the degree of detail or specificity which these imaginative ruminations have." Sensory imagery is not essential, although its presence may heighten the act of imagination's psychological effects (Price, *Belief*, p. 343). A person does not literally form a *picture* of God, for example, but "imagine[s] God *as* being His Lord and Master, *as* being one with whom he has personal relations, and *as* being a proper object of both fear and love" (p. 348).

is largely notional for they don't appreciate evil's horror. Cosmological arguments are not likely to impress someone who is not struck by the fact that things exist when nothing might have or lacks a vivid sense of how odd it would be to discover a contingent being that had no causes whatever, and whose apprehension of "Something exists" or "Every event has a cause" is therefore notional.

But real assents depend on images (or acts of imagination), and these depend on personal experience. Because "the experience of one man is not the experience of another," real apprehension and assent "is proper to the individual and, as such, thwarts, rather than promotes, the intercourse of man with man" (*GA* 82–83). If assessment of an argument's force partly depends on real assent to its premises, consensus will be difficult to achieve.

The illative sense does not, then, provide "a common measure between mind and mind" (*GA* 82). "Explicit argumentation" concerning the merits of competing principles, assumptions, points of view, and other "starting points" and "collateral aids" to argument, is "sometimes possible to a certain extent." But "it is too unwieldy an expedient for a constantly recurring need" (*GA* 290). Even when we do resort to it, agreement is unlikely. For our supporting arguments, too, must be assessed by the illative sense, and the latter reflects "personal characteristics, in which men are in fact in essential and irremediable variance with one another." The most we can do is "point out where the difference . . . lies, how far it is immaterial, when it is worthwhile continuing an argument . . . , and when not" (*GA* 283).

Our disagreements are so intractable in fact that we can only conclude "that there is something deeper in our differences than the accident of external circumstances [experience, training, and the like]; and that we need the interposition of a Power, greater than human teaching and human argument, to make our beliefs true and our minds one" (*GA* 293).

Some disagreements, of course, are less intractable than others. The first two of our five arguments involve ordinary cumulative case reasoning. No sensible person would reject the first and no reasonable historian would cavil at the second. Our spontaneous inferences from sensory phenomena to a world of independent physical and mental objects or (according to Newman) from the phenomena of conscience to a moral governor involve *natural* dispositions to interpret the data in a certain way. But the arguments to the truth of the Catholic religion and the factory girl's argument involve what William James calls "divinations" and "instincts," and these vary from mind to mind. In cases such as these, it seems doubtful whether anything less than divine intervention can secure agreement.

Yet does not this give the game away by revealing the illative sense's subjectivity? *Truth* may not be relative (Newman clearly thinks it is not),[15] but illative reasoning surely is. And because *all* reasoning involves illation, even the most rigorous thinking appears tainted by subjectivity.

This clearly is not Newman's intention. Newman believes, for example, that good cumulative case arguments for the faith are "valid proofs." Although they cannot be "forced on the mind[s] of anyone whatever," they *are* capable of convincing anyone who "*fairly* studies" their premises (*TP* 27, my emphasis). And, in general, if one's argument is good, one will find "that, allowing for the difference of minds and of modes of speech, what convinces him, does convince others also. . . . There will be very many exceptions but those will *admit of explanation*" (*GA* 300, my emphasis). Some opposed "intuitions," for example, can be discounted because they have been created by "artificial and corrupt" social codes and practices. Others can be dismissed as expressions of raw and uncultivated human nature (*TP* 70–79). The important point is that our illative sense can be well or badly employed. If everyone were to use it rightly, most major disagreements would disappear.

The Illative Sense and Proper Functioning

The test of an argument's validity is "the judgment of those who have a *right* to judge" (*GA* 248, my emphasis). "Other beings are complete from their first existence, in that line of excellence which is allotted to them." Human beings, on the other hand, must *acquire*

---

15. He denies, for example, that apparently irresolvable disagreements reflecting different points of view "prove that there is no objective truth . . . or that we are not responsible for the associations which we attach, and the relations which we assign, to the objects of the intellect" (*GA* 293).

the excellence proper to them "by the exercise of those faculties which are" their "natural inheritance." Each person must complete "his inchoate and rudimental nature . . . out of the living elements with which his mind began to be" (GA 274). The standard of proper functioning is not furnished by how most people use their ratiocinative powers. It is determined by how those who have *perfected* them do so. What does proper functioning involve, then, and what are the tests of good illative reasoning?

Experience and practice are necessary. Those are qualified to judge "who by long acquaintance with their subject have a right to judge. And if we wish ourselves to share in their convictions and the grounds of them, we must follow their history, and learn as they have learned. We must take up their particular subject . . . give ourselves to it, depend on practice and experience more than on [formal or explicit] reasoning" (GA 269). For example, the prerequisite for assessing "We shall have a European War, for Greece is audaciously defying Turkey" is the "experience ["of diplomatists, statesmen, capitalists, and the like"] strengthened by practical and historical knowledge" (GA 241).

Moral qualifications may also be necessary. Indeed, the *only* "department of inquiry" that does not require "a special preparation of mind" is "abstract science" (GA 321). The reasoner's "moral state" is not important "in a subject-matter so [comparatively] clear and simple as astronomical science," for instance (although the *type* of thinking is the same as that employed in "soft" disciplines and in ordinary life, viz., cumulative case reasoning) (GA 253). In other areas, though, the moral state of the inquirer is crucial. For example, in assessing the prospects of war in Greece, experience and knowledge should be "controlled by self-interest" (GA 241).[16]

Moral qualifications in the narrower sense are sometimes required. The rays of truth "stream in upon us through the medium of our moral as well as our intellectual being." The "perception of its first principles which is natural to us is enfeebled, obstructed, perverted,

---

16. Presumably because (rational) self-interest induces reasoners to proceed cautiously and prudently; it prevents them from basing decisions on idle speculation, emotion, fear, hope and so on. (Emotion, hope, fear, etc., can be epistemically beneficial but they are epistemically pernicious in cases like this one.)

by allurements of sense and the supremacy of self, and, on the other hand, quickened by aspirations after the supernatural" (*GA* 247). The moral and spiritual qualities needed for successful religious inquiry, for example, are those needed for admission into God's company;[17] the ratiocinative process by which we come to know God is thus a "discipline inflicted on our minds" that molds "them into due devotion to Him when He is found" (*GA* 276). Again, the mind's "safeguard [against error and superstition] . . . is a right state of heart . . . holiness, or dutifulness, or the new creation, or the spiritual mind, however we word it. . . . It is love" (LSF 234).[18] And although a sound and sensitive conscience is needed to properly assess the evidence for natural religion, an investigation of the claims of revelation requires more. One must not only be imbued with the "opinions and sentiments" of natural religion (*GA* 323); one also must long for revelation and be firmly convinced of God's goodness. We should approach the evidence for revelation as "suppliants," not "judges." Those who "resolve to treat the Almighty" with "lawyerlike qualifications"[19] will not discern the evidence's force (*GA* 330–31).[20]

Robert Holyer has called our attention to the fact that Newman's views on the imagination's epistemic effects are ambivalent.[21] He asserts, for example, that the "brilliancy of the image" is not a suffi-

17. Cf. C. Stephen Evans, "Kierkegaard and Plantinga on Belief in God: Subjectivity as the Ground of Properly Basic Religious Beliefs," *Faith and Philosophy* 5 (1988), 25–39.

18. Newman provides only one plausible example of *how* love does this. Love precludes "the worship of evil spirits" by causing "the mind to recoil from cruelty, impurity, and the assumption of divine power, though coming with ever so superhuman a claim" (LSF 240–41).

19. "Dispassionateness, a judicial temper, clear headedness, and candour" (*GA* 331). Presumably dispassionateness and neutrality are the culprits.

20. One does not need divine assistance to assent to truths of natural religion. Everyone whose conscience is not blunted discerns them. Nor is assenting to revelation on the basis of cumulative case reasoning supernatural. What *is* supernatural (a gift of grace) is "1. the assent to the fitness of believing" (i.e., seeing that it is *good* to do so), "2. the wish to believe," and "3. the act <habit> of faith distinctly embracing and holding as true the fact of the Revelation, and the thing revealed." The latter apparently includes a determination to believe "without doubt or fear" and an assent not only to revealed propositions but to God as their "speaker" (TP 37–38). (The angle brackets enclose Newman's alternative readings and his marginal notes and corrections.) More on this in the sixth section (pp. 80–83).

21. Robert Holyer, "Religious Certainty and the Imagination: An Interpretation of J. H. Newman," *The Thomist* 50 (July 1986), 395–416.

cient reason for assent. "The natural and rightful effect of acts of imagination upon us . . . is not to create assent, but to intensify it," bringing propositions home to us so that they stir our emotions and activate our wills (GA 81). But he also suggests that imagination has a proper role to play in eliciting assent. "Real ratiocination and present imagination" should infuse our inferential processes "in order to their due exercise" (GA 250). The factory girl argument is a case in point. The "image" in the argument is the narrative that includes it. The function of the image is "to show very clearly the relation of the emotions experienced by the girl, the beliefs implicit in them, and the conclusion about God." Most of us have experienced these emotions to some degree but without seeing their relation to belief in God. "The narrative makes this relationship clear by giving us a very obvious example of it."[22] I have argued that real assents to an argument's premises are sometimes needed to appreciate its force. But real assents depend on imagination, and the latter can be lively or weak, cultivated or undisciplined. Newman believed that "one important effect of living a religious life is that it schools the imagination" and emotions.[23] By doing so, it enhances our capacity to appreciate the force of religious arguments.

How does one know when one is using one's illative powers properly? There are (at least) three indications that one is doing so. The first is "the agreement of many private judgments in one and the same view" (GA 248). Newman says, for example, that his argument from conscience would not be "worthwhile my offering it unless what I felt myself agreed with what is felt by hundreds and thousands besides me" (GA 318). In matters of religion, ethics, metaphysics, and the like, "each of us can [ultimately] speak only for himself. . . . He brings together his reasons and relies on them, because they are his own, and this is his primary" and indeed his "best evidence." Nevertheless, if it "satisfies him, it is likely to satisfy others" provided that his reasoning is sound and his conclusion true. "And doubtless he does find . . . that allowing for the difference of minds and modes of speech, what convinces him, does convince

22. Ibid., pp. 411-12.
23. Ibid., p. 415.

others also." Their agreement is "a second ground of evidence" (*GA* 300-31). (The first is one's reasons.) *Universal* agreement should not be expected because people's illative senses are often undeveloped or misemployed. A failure to secure *substantial* agreement, on the other hand, indicates that one's illative powers are being used idiosyncratically.

Other signs that one has drawn the right conclusion are "objections overcome, . . . adverse theories neutralized, . . . difficulties gradually clearing up," consistency with other things known or believed, and the fact that "when the conclusion is assumed as an hypothesis, it throws light upon a multitude of collateral facts, accounting for them, and uniting them together in one whole" (*GA* 254, 255-56). A sign that one has reasoned rightly, in other words, is that one's argument satisfies the criteria for inferences to the best explanation.

Successful practice is a further indication that our reasoning is sound. In the absence of other indicators sufficient to warrant certainty, "our only test is the *event* or experience. Hence the proverbs 'The proof of the pudding' etc., etc." (*TP* 92).[24]

---

24. There is an ambiguity in Newman that is worth noting although not important for our purposes. Informal reasoning, like all reasoning, can go wrong in two ways. Its "antecedent" may be false or delusive or its inferences invalid. But reasoning from improper antecedents is no more a failure of illative reason in the strict sense than reasoning from false premises is a failure of one's deductive powers. "Intuition" must be distinguished from reasoning. "There is a faculty in the mind which acts as a complement to reasoning, and as having truth for its direct object thereby secures its use for rightful purposes. This faculty, viewed in its relation to religion, is . . . the moral sense; but it has a wider subject matter than religion, and a more comprehensive office and scope, as being 'the apprehension of first principles,' and Aristotle has taught me to call it nous or the *noetic* faculty" (*TP* 152–53). Reason is used rightly when "its antecedents are chosen rightly by the divinely enlightened mind, being such as intuitions [i.e., "the apprehension of first principles"], dictates of conscience, the inspired Word, the decisions of the Church, and the like." It is used wrongly "when its antecedents are determined by pride, self-trust, unbelief, human affection, narrow self-interest, bad education," and so on (*TP* 154). If reason habitually starts from false premises, "the mind will be in a state of melancholy disorder." Nevertheless, reason *as such* is not subverted because "an enemy of the truth has availed itself of it for evil purposes" (*TP* 142–43) It seems to me, however, that in the *Grammar* "intuitions" and the "dictates of conscience" are sometimes included within the scope of the illative sense.

Three Objections

This section discusses three difficulties. The first two are not serious. The third is.

1. Newman believes that illative reasoning cannot be formally represented. Jay Newman claims that this is obfuscating. The factory girl argument, for example, can be represented as follows:

> Either my life is meaningless, or there is a God to wipe
> away all tears from all eyes.
> Life is not meaningless.
> Ergo.[25]

Again, "in arriving at or confirming the conclusion that Britain is an island, we may make complex deductions as well as complex inductions. . . . We can produce dozens of [formal] arguments" for the conclusion. For example, " 'I have examined over a thousand' maps and they have 'misled me on less than 1 per cent of the occasions that I have relied on them.' This map of the world indicates that Britain is an island. Ergo." Or, "Almost everything Uncle Paul has told me is true. Uncle Paul told me that Britain is an island. Therefore, etc."[26] Or again, in commenting on the example of the person who ascertains the authorship of an anonymous publication on the basis of its style, manner, and so on, Jay Newman claims that "after some introspection and reflection," he *could* "start to enumerate the main considerations that led him to his judgment."[27]

Several comments are in order. First, that our reasoning *can* be cast in the form of an inductive or deductive argument (or a complex set of them),[28] does not imply that our reasoning *had* that form. (Just as the fact that I can provide reasons for my believing Mary does not imply that my justified belief in what Mary told me was *based* on

---

25. Jay Newman, "Cardinal Newman's 'Factory-Girl Argument,' " *Proceedings of the American Catholic Philosophical Association* 46 (1972), 71–77.

26. Jay Newman, *The Mental Philosophy of John Henry Newman* (Waterloo, Ontario: Wilfred Laurier University Press, 1986), pp. 150–51.

27. Ibid., p. 157.

28. Which Newman does not deny.

those reasons.) Second, the three arguments we are now discussing (or at least the last two of them) are *best* represented as inferences to the best explanation and not as deductive or inductive arguments.[29] Third, the validity of these arguments, and of other inferences to the best explanation, does not depend on our ability to recast them in deductive or inductive form.

In any case, Jay Newman's objection misses the point. *Even if* all the considerations in cases like the third can be recovered and represented (which I doubt), and *even if* all three arguments can be recast in a deductive or inductive mode, the effective *deployment* of the formal representations depends on illation. As Newman argues, an exercise of the illative sense is needed to grasp a formal argument's *force*. (A word of caution by William G. Ward is also in order. Replacing informal arguments with formal equivalents can sometimes be dangerous. For a person may "calamitously misapprehend the balance of the reasons *pro* and *con* from the very probable circumstance, that those facts which tell on one side may be far more easily put into shape, or are far more precisely located in his memory, than those (legitimately preponderating) facts which tell on the other.")[30]

2. In an otherwise sympathetic article, Robert Holyer suggests that an argument's imaginative force can be easily confused with its logical force. When a proof appeals to the imagination, "the degree of conviction" it "inspire[s] is in excess of the logical force of the argument."[31] All that the factory girl argument *strictly* establishes, for example, is a *need* to believe in God.[32]

---

29. That is, as statistical extrapolations, inferences from past regularities, and so on.

30. William Ward, "The Reasonable Basis of Certitude," in *The Ethics of Belief Debate*, ed. Gerald D. McCarthy (Atlanta, Ga.: Scholars Press, 1986), p. 177. The essay originally appeared in the *Nineteenth Century* (1878).

31. Hoyler, "Religious Certainty," p. 411.

32. Newman's suggestion that "an uncertain or unsound <imperfect> argument," like the design argument, may have been chosen by God "to bring the multitude, as by the imagination, to a truth which logic and metaphysics cannot reach, but which they could know in no other way" (*TP* 162) could be read as supporting Holyer's contention. I think it more likely, however, that what Newman intends to say is that imaginatively grasping "imperfect" arguments like these can provide epistemic access to God. "Imperfect" may simply mean "lacks the demonstrative force that metaphysicians require of their arguments."

This suggestion, while plausible, fails to do justice to one of Newman's most important contentions—that our imagination and needs
can be epistemically relevant.

Is there a gap between (e.g.) the factory girl argument's imaginative and logical force? There is *if* we identify the latter with the aver-
age force the argument has for sane and informed reasoners, or with
the force it has for those who refuse to let themselves be influenced
by the needs and emotions that the argument expresses. And it is
true that imagination and emotion can mislead us. People wrongly
"believe what they wish to be true . . . readily believe reports unfavorable to persons they dislike, or confirmations of theories of their
own." These "inducements to belief . . . prevail with all of us." Even
"faith degenerates into weakness, extravagance . . . [and] prejudice"
when "our wishes are inordinate, or our opinions are wrong" (FRC
189-90). It is also true that imagination and emotion can add force to
arguments on *both* sides of an issue—atheological arguments, for instance, as well as theological ones. Their effects are not invariably benign.

Imagination and emotion, then, seem to be one thing, reason and
intuition (the grasp of first principles), another. Newman himself
says as much. "The mind without any doubt is made for truth. Still,
it does not therefore follow that truth is its object in all its powers.
The imagination is a wonderful faculty in the cause of truth, but it
often subserves the purposes of error—so do our most innocent affections" (*TP* 152).

The *Grammar*, on the other hand, contends that the illative reasoning that is utilized in the deployment and appraisal of *all* arguments, even formal ones, is unavoidably suffused with imagination,
emotion, and need. Newman's final opinion appears to be that this is
as it should be. "Real ratiocination and present imagination" should
infuse the processes of (informal) inference "in order to their due exercise" (*GA* 250).

Note that we often use epistemic terms to appraise acts of imagination. They can be profound, insightful, or perceptive. Their prod-
ucts can have the ring of truth, place reality in a new and revealing
light, and so on, or, on the contrary, be shallow, ring false, or distort
reality. That the imagination and emotions can be misused does not

imply that, when *properly* used, they cannot have positive epistemic value. What is needed is a critique of the imagination and emotions—an account of when they are epistemically beneficial and when harmful. We are not totally in the dark. Appreciation of evil's horror, for instance, is needed to grasp the force of the argument from evil. If Christian theism is correct, however, it can be excessive or (perhaps more accurately) can unduly occupy the imagination to the exclusion of other appropriate emotions and images—trust, for example, or Christ as the image of God's love. In other cases, images and emotions that make atheological arguments persuasive to some may be *in*appropriate. Possible examples are narratives like Butler's *The Way of All Flesh* or the pictures of Christianity painted by Thomas Paine and other deists.[33]

Is there a gap between an argument's imaginative and its logical force? There need not be if (1) an argument's logical force is the force it *should* have for sane and informed reasoners, and (2) a properly disciplined imagination and emotion *should* infuse the processes of inference "in order to their due exercise." To simply *assume* that (2) is false begs the question.

Nor can one just assume that *needs* are epistemically irrelevant. Holyer argues that what the factory girl argument strictly proves is not the conclusion but that we need to believe it. The alleged gap would be illusory, however, if this need were epistemically relevant. It is reasonably clear that Newman thought it was. In a letter of 1884 to Wilfred Ward, he wrote, "it seems to me you mean to say that the same considerations which make you wish to believe are among the reasons which, when you actually do inquire, lead you prudently to believe, thus serving a double purpose. Do you bring this out anywhere? On the contrary, are you not shy of calling these considerations reasons? Why?"[34] The implication is that Newman thought they were. To simply assume that our wishes and needs are not "reasons" begs the question at issue, "Do wishes, needs, emotions, acts of imagination, and the like sometimes have positive epistemic value?"

33. Of course one would have to *show* that these images are inappropriate, that they caricature Christian life and doctrine.

34. Wilfred Philip Ward, *The Life of John Henry Cardinal Newman*, vol. 2 (London: Longmans, Green, 1912), p. 489.

3. The most serious charge is irrationalism. Jay Newman believes that Newman has "made the reasonableness of religious belief [though not its truth] a subjective matter." People's illative senses lead them to opposed conclusions, and there is not any principled way of resolving their differences. He concedes that the problem could be defused by showing that the illative senses of (e.g.) Montaigne and others who would be unimpressed by the factory girl's argument "were somehow defective." For the judgments that count are those of people "who have a right to judge" (GA 248). He doubts, however, that Montaigne is less qualified to judge her argument than the uneducated factory girl.[35] Newman of course thought that "holiness or dutifulness, or the new creation, or the spiritual mind . . . [or] love" is the qualification needed (LSF 234). But Muslims, Buddhists, and others make similar claims. They too insist that they possess a proper moral disposition, "a serious, sober, thoughtful, pure, affectionate, and devout mind" (LSF 250).[36]

The trouble with Newman's thesis is that illative reasoners cannot show that those who disagree with them are in an epistemically inferior position because they do not have any common standards to appeal to. The consequences for his claim are disastrous. If the factory girl's inference "is so personal that it has nothing to do with any common measure, standard, or rules," it can be neither valid nor invalid.[37] Nor is Newman entitled to "assume that his insight is 'deeper' and 'more powerful' than [say] Gibbon's" if he is not "prepared to produce the explicit, verbal, publicly assessable arguments that will resolve the dispute."[38]

While a full reply to this objection must await Chapter 4, three observations are in order.

(1) Whether all inference is rule governed or not depends on how "rules" is understood. It is not, if by "rules" we mean "algorithms." There are no algorithms for testing inferences to the best explanation. And though the selection of scientific paradigms is governed by what Thomas Kuhn calls "scientific values" (simplicity, comprehen-

---

35. Jay Newman, "Cardinal Newman's 'Factory-Girl Argument,' " pp. 74–75.
36. Jay Newman, *The Mental Philosophy of John Henry Newman*, p. 84.
37. Ibid., p. 153.
38. Ibid., p. 175.

siveness, precision, etc.), there are no mechanical decision procedures that a scientist can use to demonstrate the superiority of her choice. In the absence of algorithms, however, rational men and women can arrive at opposed conclusions without obvious error. (More on this in Chapter 5.).

(2) Jay Newman appears to believe that one has no right to trust one's judgment unless one can convince (all or most) informed and intelligent people of its soundness. Newman, for example, has no right to trust the factory girl's argument if he cannot convince people like Montaigne of its correctness. This (as I shall argue in Chapter 4) sets an impossibly high standard. It implies, for example, that we have no right to beliefs on philosophically disputed matters. It also assumes that the special qualifications that Newman believes we need to discern the argument's force are epistemically irrelevant. Newman thinks that people like Montaigne fail to appreciate the argument because their conscience and religious sensibilities have been blunted. To assume that the argument must convince *every* informed and intelligent reasoner implies that this qualification is not epistemically required. The assumption is therefore question-begging.

(3) Jay Newman correctly points out that the Christian's opponents, too, can appeal to special qualifications. But what follows? That he will not be able to convince everyone? That he cannot provide a non-question-begging defense of his epistemic position? Probably. Whether these consequences are disastrous, though, depends on whether it is reasonable to require universal agreement or non-question-begging justifications of basic epistemic practices. I have suggested that the first sets an impossibly high standard. William Alston has shown that the second does so as well.[39] Sense perceptual practices, for instance, cannot be justified without epistemic circularity.

Even if these points are granted, however, disagreement among illative reasoners—and the role passion, need, and emotion play in reasoning—are troublesome. Why, when all is said and done, *should* we trust our illative powers? Why think they are reliable? We will address this question in the next section.

---

39. See, for example, his "Epistemic Circularity," *Philosophy and Phenomenological Research* 47 (1986), 1–30.

The Reliability of the Illative Sense

It is essential to Newman's position that illative reasoning be natural. (This is why he wants to demonstrate its pervasiveness.) Epistemic positions that ignore the way in which the mind actually works
are empty. An evidentialist such as Locke, for example, insists on *stateable* evidence, demands that arguments be based on *universally* received
premises, and so on. But in doing so, Locke is governed by "his own
ideal of how the mind ought to act, instead of interrogating human
nature, as an existing thing, as it is found in the world." This is an
error, for an examination of the mind as an existing fact is needed not
only to discover what "our constitutive faculties" are actually like but
also to determine "our *proper* condition" (*GA* 139, my emphasis).
Newman assumes that our "own living personal reason" can be in either a "healthy" or unhealthy condition (*GA* 239). He says, for example, that the "supra-logical judgment, which is the warrant for our
certitude about" conclusions "throughout the range of concrete matter" is an expression of "the true healthy action of our ratiocinative
powers" (*GA* 251). But he also notes that our epistemic powers can be
"enfeebled, obstructed, perverted, by allurements of sense and the supremacy of self" (*GA* 247). Indeed, in "ordinary minds," they are
often "biased and degraded by prejudice, passion and self-interest"
(*GA* 261). The following example illustrates these points.

Because God's hand in nature and human affairs is hidden, it is
"possible without absurdity to deny His will, His attributes, His existence." But the reason we only "glean . . . faint and fragmentary
glimpses of Him" is that we are "alienated from Him" (*GA* 309–10).
The minds of those who believe "in God and in a future judgment,"
on the other hand, "are in the normal condition of human nature"
(*GA* 379). Conscience is part of our natural noetic equipment and
(when it has not been blunted) clearly witnesses to God. A person
whose conscience is sensitive will also assess the evidence for revelation differently from one whose conscience is not. Those who feel
no need of a revelation will "come to the examination . . . as calmly
and dispassionately as if they were judges in a court of law, or inquiring into points of science" (FWS 21). A person who desires and
needs a revelation, on the other hand, "will show his caution" and

prudence in believing and obeying, even though the revelation "might be more clearly attested. If it is but slightly probable that rejection of the Gospel will involve his eternal ruin," he judges it "safest and wisest to act as if it were certain" (FWS 23).

Which attitude is proper? The need of and desire for a revelation are natural effects of conscience. We crave to know more clearly the one who speaks to us in conscience, and guilt cries out for atonement. Because a sensitive conscience is natural and proper, so too are this need and desire.

But how do we know that a sensitive conscience is natural and proper? And more generally, how do we know when the mind is functioning as it ought? Not just by learning how people reason, for they often reason badly. "Reason actually and historically," "reason in the educated intellect of England, France, and Germany," and indeed in "every civilization through the world which is under the influence of the European mind," "reason in fact and concretely in fallen man," is perverted by false principles (TP 143). How, then, discover the nature of proper functioning? Newman's answer is not clear but seems to be: "By determining what uses of our powers contribute to human flourishing." A thing's natural powers are "suitable to it, and subserve its existence." Each species find its "good in the use" of its "particular nature" (GA 273). If it does, then our faculties are functioning properly when they contribute to our well-being. Because a developed conscience is essential to human flourishing, a belief in God and an openness to revelation (which are natural effects of conscience) are expressions of properly functioning epistemic capacities.

An examination of the way in which we actually think shows that illative reasoning is natural, for "that is to be accounted a normal operation of our nature, which men in general do actually instance" (GA 270). Our illative capacities, then, are part of our natural noetic equipment. Yet why should we trust them? For three reasons. The first is "necessity." "Our being, with its faculties . . . is a fact not admitting of question, all things being of necessity referred to it, not it to other things." Indeed, "there is no medium between using my faculties, as I have them, and flinging myself upon the external world according to the random impulse of the moment" (GA 272).

The second is "interest." "It is a general law that, whatever is found as a function or attribute of any class of beings, or is natural to it, is in its substance suitable to it and subserves its existence." Each species thus finds its "good" in the use of its "particular nature" (GA 273). Because illative reasoning is natural to us, its proper use subserves our existence and contributes to our good.

The third reason is providence. "The laws of the mind are the expression, not of a mere constituted order, but of His will" (GA 275). "*A Good Providence* watches over us" and "blesses such means of argument as it has pleased Him to give us . . . if we use them duly for those ends for which He has given them" (GA 320–21). Confident in the divine providence, "we may securely take them as they are, and use them as we find them" (GA 275).[40]

---

40. In *Skepticism and Reasonable Doubt: The British Naturalist Tradition in Wilkens, Hume, Reid, and Newman* (Oxford: The Clarendon Press, 1986), M. Jamie Ferreira argues that Newman came to believe that we *could not* (coherently) mistrust our faculties; talk of "trusting" them is therefore misplaced. As a result, whereas Newman had once grounded our faculties' reliability in a belief in Providence, he effectually ceased to do so in the *Grammar*. To support this contention Ferreira cites four passages. (a) "I should be bound by them ["the laws of the mind"] even if they were not His laws" (GA 275). (b) "First principles come *either* 'from heaven, *or* from the nature of things, *or* from the nature of man' " (Ferreira, *Skepticism*, p. 222, her emphasis. The internal quote is from Newman, *The Present Position of Catholics in England* [London: Longmans, Green, 1908], p. 293). (c) "It is enough for the proof of the value and authority of any function which I possess, to be able to pronounce that it is natural" (GA 273). (d) "That is to be accounted a normal operation of our nature, which men in general do actually instance. That is a law of our minds, which is exemplified in action on a large scale, whether a priori it ought to be a law or no" (GA 270). I do not find this convincing. (1) The necessity of using our faculties may make (the practice of) skepticism *pragmatically* irrational; it does not make it *epistemically* irrational. Nor is it clear that Newman thought that it did. (2) That a practice is natural (necessary) could be a sufficient epistemic warrant even if four faculties would *not* have been trustworthy if God had not created them. For if God *has* created them, that they are operating normally is a sufficient condition for trusting them. B can be a sufficient condition of C even if A is a sufficient condition of B's being a sufficient condition of C and B would not have been a sufficient condition of C if not-A. ($B \to C$, $A \to [B \to C]$, and not-$A \to$ not-$[B \to C]$ can all be true.) (3) The most straightforward reading of the *Grammar* is that Newman thought there were *several* grounds for trusting our faculties, each of which is sufficient. (4) The passages Ferreira cites are inconclusive. (d) does not clearly say *anything* about the *reliability* of our faculties. (b) and (c) are perfectly compatible with my interpretation. (The disjunction in [b] need not be read exclusively.) (a) could be read as asserting that I would be forced to rely on my faculties (in which case doing so would be pragmatically rational), even if God had not created them.

How convincing is this? David Pailin argues that even though "illation is natural, it is still liable to err. This liability declines as our experience and practice increase but it never completely disappears. The practice of illation, therefore, does not confirm Newman's general justification of its fidelity by reference to its naturalness, and to the blessings of divine Providence."[41] As it stands, Pailin's contention is false. Some liability to error is compatible with a faculty's general reliability. As Newman says, it is natural (and reasonable) to trust the senses, even though we know they sometimes deceive us. "Again, we [rightly] rely implicitly on our memory, and that, too, in spite of its being obviously unstable and treacherous. . . . The same remarks apply to our assumption of the fidelity of our reasoning powers" (FR 213–14).

It is true, though, that a noetic faculty should be distrusted if the *trained* capacity is *prone* to error. Wide disagreement among those with *cultivated* noetic capacities would be a clear indication of unreliability. Newman implicitly agrees; properly functioning noetic equipment should lead to widespread agreement. "If religion," for example, "is consequent upon *reason* and at the same time for *all* men, there must be reasons producible sufficient for the rational conviction of every individual" (TP 86). Furthermore, "since the grounds are to be such as apply to all classes of men, they must lie deep in the constitution of our nature." They must also "be obvious and not abstract: of a natural persuasiveness, of a nature to be intelligible to and to arrest the attention of all, and to touch them and come home to them, and work upon them" (TP 87). (Although he does not say so, Newman is clearly thinking of conscience.)

Properly used noetic faculties attain truth for the most part. "Assents to things as true, made under a sense of duty, and the guidance of the judgment, generally succeed in having <attaining> a true object" or "objects in substance true, however they may be coloured, or distorted, or maimed, or . . . leavened with falsehood" (TP 121–22). A widespread failure in attaining "objects in substance true" thus calls for explanation. But Newman of course has one. Religious disagreement, for instance, is explained by blunted consciences and,

41. Pailin, *Way of Faith*, p. 150.

ultimately, original sin. Whether these explanations can be defended
without circularity is another matter.

The problem of circularity also arises in another connection. If
illative reasoning is necessary, we are pragmatically justified in employing it. Ought implies can. If illative reasoning is unavoidable, I
cannot be faulted for engaging in it. That it is in my interest is another reason for thinking that illative reasoning is practically or pragmatically rational. But is it *epistemically* reasonable? Does it track the
truth? It is, and does, if it is an "expression . . . of His will." For God
is not a deceiver.

Yet how do I *know* that my noetic capacities are a gift of providence? By deploying my illative capacities. "Since one of their very
functions is to tell me of Him, they throw a reflex light upon themselves" (*GA* 275). By employing them, I learn of God's providence
and thus acquire a reason for trusting them. The *force* of this reason,
however, is not clear. For there is an obvious circularity; my justification employs the capacities whose credentials are in question. Whether
circles of this kind are vicious will be discussed in Chapter 4.

Newman and Evidentialism

Evidentialists such as Locke think that religious beliefs are not rationally held unless they are based on good evidence. Newman's position is closer to evidentialism than his criticism of Locke suggests.

He clearly thinks that faith is *rational*. "Faith must rest on reason,
nay even in the case of children and of the most ignorant and dull
peasant, wherever faith is living and loving" (*TP* 86). Yet is faith an
expression of reason*ing*? Is it, in other words, based on evidence?
Some passages suggest not. Faith is swayed "by its own hopes, fears,
and existing opinions" as well as by "the actual evidence producible
in its favour" (FRC 187–88). And in commenting on the definition
of faith in *Hebrews*, Newman says, "its desire [i.e., hope] is its main
evidence; or . . . makes its own evidence . . . not that it has no
grounds in Reason, that is, in evidence; but because it is satisfied
with so much less than would be necessary, were it not for the bias
of the mind, that to the world its evidence seems like nothing"
(FRC 190–91). Or again, "faith . . . is an . . . exercise of Reason"

which has "grounds besides" "the actual evidence" (FR 207–08). Although faith is rational, it seems to go beyond the evidence.

But the impression these passages create is misleading, for by "actual evidence," Newman means evidence that is easily stateable and widely accessible; faith's reasonings may appear illogical to the skeptic but only because "the subject matter" is "more or less special and recondite" and "the premises undeveloped" (FR 208). "Faith . . . does not demand evidence so strong as is necessary for what is *commonly* considered a rational conviction . . . and why? . . . because it is mainly swayed by antecedent considerations . . . previous notices, prepossessions, and (in a good sense of the word) prejudices" rather than by "direct and definite proof" (FRC 187, my emphasis). These "prejudices" and "prepossessions" determine our view of prior probabilities and the evidence's weight. For "probabilities have no definite ascertained value, and are reducible to no scientific standard, what are such to each individual," therefore, "depends on his moral temperament. . . . Man is [thus] responsible for his faith, because he is responsible for his likings and dislikings, his hopes and his opinions, on all of which his faith depends" (FRC 191–92).

Newman's position appears to be this. Faith rests on evidence. But some of it cannot be easily recovered or stated, and the evidence as a whole is likely to seem weak to those with some moral temperaments. Newman is *not* an evidentialist if evidentialism requires stateable and publicly accessible evidence that compels assent regardless of a person's moral temper. Evidentialists have usually insisted on evidence of this kind. Newman nonetheless believes that properly formed religious beliefs are based on (sufficient) evidence, and that those whose noetic faculties are functioning as they should will find this evidence convincing.

Newman's contribution to the tradition Edwards represents is his demonstration that the way in which the mind reasons when influenced by religious sentiments, images, and ideas is the way in which it reasons on ordinary occasions. "Moral evidence and moral certitude are all that we can attain, not only in the case of ethical and spiritual subjects, such as religion, but of terrestrial and cosmical [i.e., scientific] questions also" (GA 252). In both cases reasoners employ cumulative case arguments or inferences to the best explanation. Although it is true that the "moral state of the parties inquiring or disputing" is not relevant in subjects such as astronomy (*GA* 253), its relevance is *not* restricted to "spiritual subjects," for passional factors play a role in historical inquiry, philosophy, and everyday reasoning. If the way in which theists assess evidence is suspect, then so too is the way in which historians, philosophers, and ordinary practical reasoners do so, for their procedures are essentially similar. The theist's critics, therefore, must either discredit the sort of thinking that goes on in cases such as these or provide *special* reasons for believing that the theist's sentiments, modes of imagination, and ideas are suspect, that is, that the moral state that leads to *positive* assessments of the theistic evidence is likely to impair reasoning rather than to enhance it.

There is one significant difference from Edwards. If I understand Newman correctly, supernatural principles are not needed to grasp (any) religious truths.

Newman calls the kind of religious belief we have been discussing "fides acquisita" or "fides humana" and distinguishes it from "fidis divina" (*TP* 38). The latter involves not only "an opinion or the belief about an alleged fact or truth" but also "a determination <maintenance/belief> that it can not be otherwise <never to think otherwise/that belief will continue>" (*TP* 7). That is, it implies the absence of fear as well as doubt. One not only has no present doubts; one has no fear that the evidence will fail one in the future. Divine faith thus involves "a transcendent adhesion of mind, intellectual and moral, and a special self-protection, beyond the operation of . . . ordinary laws of thought" (*GA* 156). It also "follows on a divine announcement" (*GA* 156). *Human* faith "does not *necessarily* suppose a speaker" (*TP* 38), but faith "in its theological sense" believes things "because God has revealed them" (*GA* 94). Divine faith thus involves a divinely assisted commitment firmly to maintain one's assent or certitude in the face of any doubts that may arise, and an assent to the propositions one believes *as* revealed, that is, one assents to them as one assents to what a deeply trusted friend tells one.[42]

---

42. This should be distinguished from assenting to a proposition because one has good evidence that one's friend or some other trustworthy person has asserted it.

Human and divine faith are both expressions of reason, and the type of reasoning and evidence are the same in both cases. In instances of divine faith, God strengthens the will (the resolve to maintain belief in the face of pressure and doubt) and enables the mind to assent to propositions as revealed. But he does not (as far as I can see) supply the mind with new data like the simple idea of true beauty.[43] Furthermore, *all* religious dogmas are accessible to natural reason because natural reason can be firmly convinced that they have been revealed and should therefore be believed. The difference between human and divine faith is thus a difference in the *manner* of belief, and not in its content, its evidence, or the process of reasoning by which it is formed. In *this* sense religious knowing is "naturalized." Even if charity (and thus a new supernatural principle) is needed to appreciate the *full* force of the evidence for revelation, divine faith does not involve a "new sense of the heart" or "spiritual perception."[44]

43. I am assuming that assenting to a proposition *as* revealed does not involve a new quasi-perceptual awareness of the divine revealer; if it does, divine faith involves new data. However, as Newman describes it, assenting to a proposition as revealed seems more like a gestalt switch than a new perception.

44. Newman's account of divine faith's *epistemic* (as distinguished from its moral and spiritual) dimension is thus essentially the same as Edwards's account of religious beliefs which are expressions of *common* grace.

[3]
William James, Rationality, and Religious Belief

One of William James's earliest philosophical essays sounds a note that echoes throughout his writings. Criticizing Spencer's definition of truth as ("mere") correspondence, James asserts that a "correspondence" between the mind and reality is a "*right* mental action," and rightness is determined by "pure *subjective interests* . . . brought . . . upon the scene and corresponding to no relation already there" (*EP* 11).[1]

It is important to appreciate how pervasive interest is. Science itself is an expression of it. Its concepts are formed by abstracting selected aspects of reality, and selection is determined by interests. The "essences" or "kinds" of philosophy and science are "purely teleo-

1. References in this chapter are to the following works of James unless otherwise noted. *Essays in Philosophy* (Cambridge: Harvard University Press, 1978), hereafter *EP*; *Essays in Religion and Morality* (Cambridge: Harvard University Press, 1982), hereafter *ERM*; "The Dilemma of Determinism," "Is Life Worth Living?," "The Sentiment of Rationality," "Reflex Action and Theism," and "The Will to Believe," in *The Will to Believe and Other Essays in Popular Philosophy* (New York, c. 1896; reprint, New York: Dover, 1956), hereafter DD, Life, SR, RAT, and WTB, respectively; *The Meaning of Truth* (New York, 1907; reprint, Cambridge: Harvard University Press, 1975), hereafter *MT*; *Pragmatism* (New York, 1907; reprint, New York: Meridian Books, 1955), hereafter Prag; *The Principles of Psychology*, 2 vols. (New York, 1890; reprint, New York: Dover, 1950), hereafter *Principles*; *A Pluralistic Universe* (New York, 1909; reprint, New York: Longmans, Green, 1947), hereafter *PU*; *Some Problems in Philosophy* (New York, 1911; reprint, Cambridge: Harvard University Press, 1979), hereafter *SPP*; and *The Varieties of Religious Experience* (New York: The Modern Library, c. 1902), hereafter *VRE*.

logical weapons of the mind. The essence of a thing is that one of its properties which is *so important for my interests* that in comparison with it, I may neglect the rest." (*Principles* II 335). Scientific Values— "usefulness . . . 'elegance' . . . congruity with our residual beliefs," the desire for a "cleaner, clearer, more inclusive mental view"—are "subjective qualities" (*MT* 41–42). Even the demand for successful predictions ("uniformity of sequence") is "as subjective and emotional" as my other demands because it is an expression of the practical need "in a general way at least, [to] banish uncertainty from the future" (DD 147; SR 77).

Assessments of scientific evidence are also affected by interests. Two scientists may draw different conclusions from the same body of evidence because each "is peculiarly sensitive to evidence that bears in some one direction." In these cases, their conclusions ultimately reflect "a sort of dumb conviction that the truth must lie in one direction rather than another" (SR 92–93).

James's point, in short, is not just that science *serves* an interest (the acquisition of new truths, technical mastery, and so on); the scientific enterprise is *intrinsically infused* with them. Nevertheless, science *is* dominated by our "theoretic needs" and differs in this respect from other forms of human inquiry.

The "theoretic need," however, is "but one of a thousand human purposes" (SR 70). Some of these play a more prominent role in other disciplines such as metaphysics.

The "objective" facts are not decisive. Comprehensive metaphysical systems such as idealism and materialism conflict, and "objective nature[2] has contributed to both sides impartially" (*PU* 23). If we can "suppose for a moment that both give a conception of equal theoretic clearness and consistency, and that both determine our expectations equally well," our choice will be determined by passion and interest (SR 89).

In the final analysis, our visions of the world are "accidents more or less of personal vision" (*PU* 10), for they express our "temperament"—our "individual way of just seeing and feeling the total push

---

2. Roughly, the generally admitted facts of science and common sense; the facts about which there is no real dispute.

and pressure of the cosmos" (*Prag.* 18). Absolute idealism, for example, ultimately rests on a "generous vital enthusiasm about the universe" and a will that things "*shall* cohere . . . *shall* be one" (*PU* 140, 143). The "tough-minded" find materialism compelling, but the "tender-minded" find it unsatisfactory. A pluralism that places great importance on human moral capacities is an expression of days in which we are "in the full and successful exercise of our moral energy," and "the life we . . . feel tingling through us vouches sufficiently for itself." Religious monism, on the other hand, is rooted in days when we are " 'all sicklied o'er' with the sense of weakness, of helplessness, failure and of fear" (*ERM* 61–62).

The influence of passion and need is not occasional or accidental. James clearly thinks that *every* worldview is partially determined by it and that *no* worldview seems compelling in its absence.

The question, then, is not whether interests suffuse and shape our intellectual enterprises, for they clearly do. It is whether interests *should* do so—whether their influence *vitiates* inquiry and, in particular, whether the dominant role need and passion play in metaphysics makes metaphysical choices *nonrational*. James thinks it sometimes does not; metaphysical beliefs *are* sometimes rational. The question is, "Rational in what sense?"

Passion and Evidence

"The Will to Believe" describes a set of circumstances in which people are justified in embracing beliefs that are not self-evident or adequately supported by "objective" evidence. Two conditions must be met.

First, the choice between the belief and its alternatives is "living," "momentous," and "forced." The choice is living if each alternative "appeals as a real possibility to him to whom it is proposed"—that is, if one has some inclination to believe and thus act on it (*WTB* 2). For example, the choice between determinism and indeterminism is a living option for many of us because we have some tendency to believe in determinism and some tendency to deny it.

A choice is momentous if the opportunity presented is unique, the stake is significant, and the decision is irreversible "if it later prove unwise." James's example is a person who has the opportunity of going on a long polar expedition. The opportunity will not recur. He wishes to go but will have to sacrifice other interests to do so and, once embarked, he cannot go back (WTB 4).

The choice is forced if it is unavoidable. "Call my theory true or call it false" does not present me with a forced option because I can do neither. But "Either accept this truth or go without it" does. I may deny it or suspend judgment. But in either case I go without it.

Second, the issue "cannot by its nature be decided on intellectual grounds" (WTB 11).[3]

James thinks that the choice between the religious hypothesis and its denial meets these conditions. Most of us have some tendency to believe the religious hypothesis and some tendency to deny it. The choice is thus living.

It is also momentous, for "we are supposed to gain, even now, by our belief, and to lose by our non-belief, a certain vital good" (WTB 26).[4] Furthermore, the choice is forced "so far as that good goes" since one loses the good, if there is one, whether one rejects the religious hypothesis as false or merely suspends judgment. (The choice presented to us is not "Call the religious hypothesis true or call it false" but "Accept it or go without it—that is, live in accordance with it or don't.")

The truth or falsity of the religious hypothesis is not self-evident. James also thinks that the objective evidence is inconclusive. The issue cannot be decided, then, on intellectual grounds.

Both conditions are thus met. We are therefore within our intellectual rights in believing the religious hypothesis.

3. When the "subjective method" was first introduced, James restricted it to cases involving facts that include a "personal contribution on our part" ("Quelques Considérations sur la méthode subjective" [1878], EP 335). This restriction is implicitly lifted in later essays. The subjective method is also legitimate when a belief is needed to secure experiences that verify it. The conditions for legitimately exercising our right to believe that are specified in WTB do not limit it to cases involving facts that depend on our actions, although these provide the most obvious counterexamples to Clifford.

4. Although the choice is clearly significant, is it unique and irreversible? Can I not postpone the decision or reverse it once I have made it? Perhaps uniqueness and irreversibility are important only because they sometimes contribute to the significance of our choices.

Belief in these circumstances is primarily an expression of will rather than intellect. But by "will" James means something broader than "choice." I cannot choose to believe just anything I please. I cannot decide to believe that I have 100 dollars in my pocket and find myself believing it. I have no tendency to believe it (partly because I know the evidence is against it) and cannot make myself believe it by trying. What, then, does James mean?

Belief in metaphysical hypotheses such as indeterminism or supernaturalism (or their opposites) is an expression of our "willing" or "passional" nature as well as our intellect; it reflects our temperament, needs, concerns, fears, hopes, passions, and emotions. Choice (conscious volition) can play a role in the formation of these beliefs. For example, we might deliberately decide to commit ourselves to the religious hypothesis or to nurture religious beliefs we already have. If deliberate choice is to be effective, however, it must be supported by our passional nature.

James's point, then, is that where the conditions for exercising our right to believe are met, we are not behaving irrationally when we follow the promptings of our willing nature.

James is often read as implying that his conditions are jointly necessary as well as sufficient. His second condition is usually construed as requiring that the evidence be evenly balanced. I suggest that both views are mistaken.

Why, for example, must the issue be forced? If a belief is momentous, live, and intellectually undecidable, why should not a person adopt it if it meets the demands of his or her passional nature? That it is or is not part of a forced option seems irrelevant.[5] ("Accept this belief or don't" is, of course, forced. This is trivial, however, for in this sense *every* belief is part of a forced option.) Nor is it clear that *both* alternatives must be live. Is it not sufficient for one alternative to be living if the other conditions are met? (James may think that, because the issue is intellectually undecidable, the absence of coercive evidence casts doubt on the preferred alternative and thereby creates a tendency to embrace the other. This is probably true of

---

5. "Irrelevant" may be too strong; if the belief is part of a forced option, I cannot *avoid* choosing and hence cannot be *faulted* for doing so.

most of us, but I doubt that it is true of those whose faith is exceptionally robust.)

Nor is it clear that the objective evidence must be equally balanced. James thought that as a matter of fact the objective evidence for and against the religious hypothesis, and for and against determinism, was evenly balanced. The evidence for pluralism, on the other hand, seemed stronger to him than the evidence for monism. Even so, he thought that "subjective factors" were needed to decide the issue *conclusively*. This suggests that James's only requirement is that the objective evidence not be "coercive."

His language supports this interpretation. He says, for example, that the question is whether we should wait for "*coercive* evidence" (WTB 22, my emphasis). He announces his intention to defend "our right to adopt a believing attitude in religious matters in spite of the fact that our merely logical intellect may not have been *coerced*" (WTB 1–2, my emphasis). He attacks the "disdain for merely *possible* or *probable* truth"—the refusal, in other words, to countenance a believing attitude in the absence of proofs that "will convince men *universally*," compelling reasons that are "absolutely impersonal," "or knockdown proofs" (*VRE* 424, 426, 428, 430, my emphases).

In short, James's only requirement seems to be that the evidence should not *clearly* or *conclusively* point in one direction rather than another. Our passional nature can thus properly come into play not only in cases in which the evidence is evenly balanced but also in those in which the objective evidence *does* incline us to one belief rather than another but where, because of the evidence's quality, our inclination to believe is inhibited by doubts and hesitations.

(Are we entitled to bring our passional nature into play when the objective evidence against the hypothesis that tempts us seems slightly *stronger* than the evidence for it? If the negative evidence is not that conclusive, it is difficult to see why not. To my knowledge, however, James never takes a position on this issue. All that is clear is that when the negative evidence *is* conclusive, we have no right to believe—presumably because experience shows that ignoring negative evidence in cases like these leads to less satisfactory relations with reality.)

James's discussions of metaphysical systems are instructive. Monism (absolute idealism), for example, provides "comfort" and permits "moral holidays." It is thus true "in so far forth." But monism also rests on an inadequate kind of logic[6] and "entangles one in metaphysical paradoxes" (*Prag.* 57–58, 60). Furthermore, it cannot explain evil or the existence of finite centers of autonomous consciousness. Finally, monism is "fatalistic"; because all facts are necessary, freedom and contingency are illusory.

Pluralism, on the other hand, is confirmed by our experience of apparent disconnections between facts and thus stays closer to "reality as perceptually experienced." It therefore claims less and so has a lighter burden of proof (*SPP* 70–74). Pluralism is also more faithful to our moral experience. Because it allows for contingency and does not "derealize" the "only life we are at home in," it makes life "seem real and earnest" (*PU* 49). It is true that monism provides more religious consolation. Nevertheless, pluralism, too, can accommodate our religious yearnings.

Reviewing these considerations, James concludes that monism should be rejected provided that its claim "that the absolute is no hypothesis but a presupposition implicated in all thinking" (*PU* 52) can be shown to be unsound.

Or consider James's defense of the "religious hypothesis." The most general form of the hypothesis has three parts.

    1. There is a "higher universe."
    2. We are better off if we believe this and act accordingly.
    3. Communion with the higher universe[7] "is a process wherein work is really done," and effects are produced in the visible world (*VRE* 475).

James also has a more specific proposal and this, too, has three parts.

    1. "The conscious person is continuous with a wider self through which saving experiences come" (*VRE* 505).

---

6. Hegelian dialectic or Bradley's logic in which what is not included in a concept is excluded by it.

7. Through prayer, meditation, devotion, commitment, and so on.

2. "Our ideal impulses originate" in another "dimension of existence"—a dimension that is not "merely ideal, for it produces effects in this world" (*VRE* 506).

3. These effects are not limited to those "exerted on the personal centers of energy of the various subjects"; because the "higher universe" includes "a larger power friendly" to us and to our "ideals," we have some assurance that the world's "tragedy is only provisional" (*VRE* 507, 515).[8]

These hypotheses are not capricious or ad hoc. To see why, consider James's proposed "science of religions."

It must first "eliminate the local and accidental from" the characterizations by which "the spontaneous intellect of man always defines the divine." It must then confront these "spontaneous religious constructions with the results of natural science" so as to "eliminate doctrines that are now known to be scientifically absurd or incongruous." Successful performance of the first two tasks leaves a "residuum" of hypotheses that are at least possible. After examining this residuum to distinguish "between what is innocent over-belief and symbolism . . . and what is to be taken literally," our hypotheses must finally be tested "in all the manners, whether negative or positive, by which hypotheses are ever tested" (*VRE* 445–46).[9]

James clearly thinks his hypotheses survive the first three tests. The first hypothesis is the common core of all religious creeds, and the second is the common core of popular religious faith. Neither hypothesis commits one to scientific absurdities, and both are to be taken literally. James also thinks his hypotheses survive the fourth test.

8. The first hypothesis is compatible with systems such as absolute idealism in which the ideal world "never bursts into the world of phenomena at particular points" but "leaves the laws of life just as naturalism finds them, with no hope of remedy in case their fruits are bad" (*VRE* 511). The second hypothesis is not.

9. I have reversed the order of James's last two tests. We surely want to distinguish symbolism from what is to be taken literally in the case of *all* the plausible hypotheses and not just (as James implies) of those that survive testing. If we do not, we will not be in a position to test them. What does the fourth test include? (James is quite unspecific.) Presumably all the tests not already employed in ruling out "doctrines now known to be scientifically absurd or incongruous"—simplicity, congruity with our other beliefs, ability to meet the demands of our willing nature, and so on.

The *objective* evidence is, admittedly, inconclusive. Apart from religious experience the most essential fact is that "the *last* word everywhere, according to purely naturalistic science, is the word of Death, the death-sentence passed by Nature on . . . everything she has made" (*ERM* 127). When we *include* religious experience, however, the balance shifts. Conversion (i.e., regeneration), saintliness, and mystical states "open out the possibility of other orders of truth" and "absolutely overthrow the pretension of non-mystical states to be the sole and ultimate dictators of what we may believe" (*VRE* 414, 418).[10]

But even though humanity's religious experience *restores* the balance, it does not tip it. Ultimately, "proofs" and "facts" are indecisive, or at least not "coercive." They only "corroborate our preexistent partialities," lending plausibility to "our passions or mystical intuitions" (*VRE* 427, 429). Each of us, in the final analysis, must still make his or her "personal venture," and these ventures will express our individual attitudes, intuitions, and tendencies to believe.[11]

It is important to note, however, that these intuitions and tendencies are *themselves* subject to philosophical scrutiny. Many of us, for example, refuse to believe because our attitudes have been shaped by a science whose outlook is "materialistic"—systematically repudiating the "personal point of view." From this perspective, religion seems "an anachronism, a case of 'survival,' an atavistic relapse" (*VRE* 480–81).

This attitude is unreasonable. Science can only provide "ideal pictures of something whose existence we do not inwardly possess but only point at outwardly." "*Full* facts," facts "of the kind to

10. Although I cannot argue this here, I believe that James thinks that mystical states should have *some* authority over nonmystics and that interpretations to the contrary are mistaken. What he denies is that they "have a right to be *absolutely* authoritative over the" nonmystic; that nonmystics have "a *duty* . . . to accept their revelations *uncritically.*" Those who are not mystics must "sift and test" them *as we sift and test "what comes from the outer world of sense"* (*VRE* 414, 417–18, my emphases). James only rejects the claim that these experiences' prima facie weight is sufficiently great to *close* the issue for nonmystics.

11. The objective evidence *does* rule out *some* hypotheses, however. James thinks, for example, that "healthy-minded" religions fudge the facts by denying the existence of (real) evil.

which all realities whatsoever must belong" are found in concrete personal experience. Only here do "we catch real fact in the making" (*VRE* 489, 492, my emphasis). All conceptualizations, including scientific ones, are simply abstractions from the richness of concrete experience. The "personal point of view" is thus essential. (These claims presuppose James's "radical empiricism.") In addition, religion's utility shows that it is not a "mere anachronism and survival" (*VRE* 497). Religious consciousness is highly useful because it is "dynamogenic." Religion "freshens our vital powers" and imparts "endurance . . . zest . . . meaning [and] enchantment" to life (*VRE* 495, 497).

James concludes that the religious hypothesis "fits the facts so easily" that our "scientific logic" should "find no plausible pretext for vetoing [our] impulse to welcome it as true" (*VRE* 501). He adds that when *he* considers the claim that "the world of sensations and of scientific laws and objects . . . [are] all," the "inward monitor of which W. K. Clifford once wrote" whispers "the word 'bosh!' " "The total expression of human experience *as I view it objectively* invincibly urges me beyond the narrow 'scientific' bounds. . . . So my *objective* and my subjective conscience *both* hold me to the over-belief which I express" (*VRE* 509, my emphasis). James claims, in short, that when he views the facts as honestly as he can, he finds himself so "impressed by the importance" of "the phenomena of religious life" that it seems most reasonable to "adopt the hypothesis which they so naturally suggest" (*VRE* 513). *Personal* idiosyncracies (of temperament, passion, outlook, etc.) are not appealed to. "Subjectivity" enters the picture only insofar as, in assessing the whole drift of the total evidence, James refuses to stifle his (and what he also believes to be humanity's) natural religious proclivities.

Notice two things. The first is the way in which James weaves so-called "objective" and "subjective" considerations together in making his case for pluralism and religion. The second is James's clear belief that decisions to embrace pluralism and the religious hypotheses are reasonable—not only in the minimal sense that believing is within our epistemic rights but also in the sense that we *should not* stifle the promptings of our passional nature that incline us to believe them.[12] But rational in what way? What kind of rationality is involved in coming to these decisions?

Three Mistaken Readings

Three readings seem mistaken. The first is John E. Smith's.[13] Some metaphysical issues can be settled by appealing to experience.[14] Others cannot. The controversies between religion and materialism, indeterminism and determinism, and meliorism and pessimism are examples. Because the hypotheses at stake are meaningful their truth can, in principle, be decided by experience. The relevant experiences, however, are not yet in. Because they are not, we are not yet in a position to resolve the issues "intellectually." But our attitudes toward these theses deeply matter. We cannot afford to postpone a decision. We are therefore entitled to transfer the issues' venue from the court of theoretic reason to the court of our passional nature.

Others assimilate James to Pascal. There *are* obvious similarities. Both insist that the issues cannot be resolved on purely intellectual grounds, and both appeal to the good at stake. It is therefore tempting to suppose that James, too, thinks we should embrace claims like the religious hypothesis because it is prudentially rational to do so.

Gerald Myers believes that James's argument is a moral one. One needs religious belief to "preserve one's own inner integrity" in the great crises of life. (It is needed to maintain the "strenuous mood," to defend oneself against pessimism, for influxes of "energy and cheerfulness," etc.). Because "the moral obligation to preserve one's own integrity" outweighs "the moral obligation to be skeptical and

12. As Peter Madden points out in his introduction to the Harvard edition of *The Will to Believe and Other Essays in Popular Philosophy*, James has a weak and strong version of his will to believe doctrine—that we have a *right* to believe either alternative in the cases in question and that, because of certain features of our passional nature, we *should* believe one alternative rather than the other. He stresses the first when speaking to the "tough-minded" and the second when speaking to the "tender-minded." On the whole, James seems committed to the stronger version.

13. John E. Smith, *Purpose and Thought: The Meaning of Pragmatism* (New Haven: Yale University Press, 1978).

14. Smith cites the monism-pluralism debate as an example. For reasons already given, I do not believe that James thinks this issue can be fully resolved without appealing to "subjective" factors.

withhold belief in the absence of supportive evidence," one not only has a right to believe, one should do so. Religious belief is "legitimate and rational."[15]

These interpretations share an assumption—that the sense in which it is sometimes rational to prefer one alternative in a living option is practical; it is existentially, or prudentially, or morally reasonable to do so. I believe this is mistaken.

James is attempting to show that we are rationally entitled to certain *beliefs* and not just that we are rationally entitled to act *as if* certain beliefs were true or to *cultivate* certain beliefs. *Believing* objectively unsupported propositions is sometimes rational and not merely attitudes and actions associated with believing. (Although James sometimes equates believing and acting as if one believed, we should not take this literally.[16] What James has in mind is adopting a "working hypothesis" [SR 95–96, EP 337]. This not only involves public advocacy, an "open application to life,"[17] and going in against alternatives like materialism "as we should *go in*, had we a chance, against the second French Empire." It also involves *expecting* things to turn out as the hypothesis says [SR 95–96]. Adopting a working hypothesis, in other words, typically involves [tentatively] thinking it *true*).[18]

I shall argue that James thinks that some passionally grounded beliefs are not only *practically* rational but also *epistemically* rational. Smith's reading is defective because it severs the link between our

15. Gerald Myers, *William James: His Life and Thought* (New Haven: Yale University Press, 1986), pp. 452–53.

16. For example, in a footnote to "The Will to Believe," James equates them on the grounds that "belief is measured by action." But note that the footnote concludes, "I myself believe . . . that the religious hypothesis gives to the world an expression which specifically determines our reactions, and makes them in large part unlike what they might be on a purely naturalistic scheme of belief" (29–30). James's remarks in other places make it clear that these reactions include not only actions but also emotions, attitudes, *and expectations*.

17. James, "Preface," The Will to Believe, pp. xi–xiii.

18. See, for example, "Faith and the Right to Believe": "If the 'melioristic' universe were *really* there, it would require the active good-will of all of us, *in the way of belief* [my emphasis] as well as of our other activities, to bring it to a prosperous issue" (SPP 115). Cf. VRE 54–55, where (in discussing Kant) James glosses acting "*as if* there were a God" or "*as if* we were to be immortal" with "our faith *that* [what Kant believes to be] these unintelligible objects actually exist."

passional nature and truth. The Pascalian interpretation is mistaken because it overlooks the fact that intellectually undecidable *beliefs* can be rational, and not merely the *act* of creating or cultivating them. Myers's reconstruction of James's argument also ignores its epistemic dimension. The only beliefs the reconstructed argument would justify are moral ones, not beliefs about what is the case.[19]

But if James *is* claiming that passionally grounded beliefs can be epistemically rational, is he not saying something preposterous? I shall argue that he is not.

Epistemic Rationality and Our Passional Nature

The aim of epistemic rationality is to increase our stock of significant truths. James never disputes this goal's overriding importance. As he says, "the concrete man has but one interest—to be right" (SR 93). The significant question is how we can best *achieve* this aim and, in particular, whether we are more likely to achieve it if we suppress the promptings of our passional nature. James thinks we are not. Scientific method is useful when it helps us achieve our goal. But if "the means presumes to frustrate the end" and some other means will help, we should employ them. "In the total game of life, we stake our persons all the while; and if *in its theoretic part* our persons will help us to a conclusion, surely we should also stake them there" (SR 93–94, my emphasis).

In James's opinion, the tendencies "in one's emotional life" can be "prophetic" (*MT* 5). Our passional nature not only consists of desires and aversions, hopes and fears. It also includes "concrete perceptions" and "insight giving passions" (*MT* 140, 141)—"instincts" (WBT 29), "divinations," "a sort of dumb conviction that the truth must lie in one direction rather than another" (SR 93), something in us that "whispers . . . 'it *must* be true' " (PU 328–29). James clearly thinks

---

19. These interpretations of James may be consistent with the claim that (e.g.) religious believers and indeterminists are within their epistemic *rights* in believing the religious hypothesis or indeterminism. (For James surely does not think that in exercising his own will to believe, he is violating an epistemic *duty*.) But they do deny that their beliefs are epistemically justified. I shall argue that this overlooks an important strand in James's thought.

that these "intuitions" or "dumb convictions" can be reliable indicators of "*theoretic*" (objective) truth.[20] Determinism, for example, is a "theoretic" hypothesis about the (objective) structure of reality. James rejects it because it "violates" his "sense of moral reality," is a "corruption of our moral sanity," and runs afoul of "instinctive reactions which" he "for one, will not tamper with" (DD 177–78).[21]

Why should we trust our passional nature? Human satisfactions are the pragmatic tests of truth or reality.[22] Because views which ignore or suppress our deepest needs and intimations are not satisfactory, they will not "ring true." Hence, to construct a picture of the world that seems rational *and true* to us, we must respect the promptings of our passional as well as of our theoretic natures.

Yet why think that our satisfactions are reliable indicators of reality or truth? James's answer seems to be this. Satisfactions and dissatisfactions are functions of a belief's ability to facilitate or hinder the exercise of the mind's vital powers. These powers, however, "are not irrelevant to" reality (SR 88). The "dumb region of the heart in which we dwell alone with our willingness and unwillingnesses, our faiths and fears" is "our deepest organ of communication with the nature of things" (Life 62). (See also "It is more than probable that to the end of time our power of moral and rational response to the nature of things will be the deepest organ of communication therewith that we shall ever possess" [RAT 141]).[23]

20. I do not mean to distinguish sharply desires and yearnings from intuitions and dumb convictions. Nor does James do so.

21. James makes it clear that the "whisper" or "instinctive reaction" should be discounted if the hypothesis in question is not really possible or is not "fit to be true."

22. Satisfactions include achieving consistency, fulfilled expectations, satisfied emotional needs, felt "congruity with our residual beliefs," and so on.

23. Cf. James's notes for "The Sentiment of Rationality": "Why is not this will, this blind substance of the living man . . . his third dimension extending from the painted surface of the intelligible world into the deep of ontology . . . why is not this absolute being?" (EP 344). James's point here may be that life, the *lebenswelt*, is the given on which all systems rest (see *Essays in Radical Empiricism* [New York: Longmans, Green, 1912]), and that it is only in willing (acting) that we "feel" life ("only not understood because above understanding") (EP 344). There is, I think, a deep connection between James's distrust of abstractions and his insistence on immersing ourselves in preconceptual experience, his enthusiasm for Bergson, and his trust in our passional nature.

Is this at all plausible? It is *if* we can assume some sort of congruence between the mind's structure and the structure of reality. That James does assume this is clearly implied in at least one place. "Reflex Action and Theism" argues that the mind has three "departments." It receives sensations, reflects on them, and discharges itself in action. No view will seem rational that violates one of these "essential modes of activity"—that neglects facts, has "a lot of inconsistencies or unmediated transitions on its hands; or else, finally . . . has left some one or more of our fundamental active and emotional powers with no [adequate] object outside of themselves to react on or to live for" (125). The key to the significance of this passage occurs earlier in the essay where James observes that a view that is not only rational (i.e., satisfying in the long run and on the whole) but also "really the living truth" must satisfy all three demands *if* "the structure of our mind . . . be in accordance with the nature of reality" (116). The whole drift of his discussion implies that James thinks that it is.

A corollary of this thesis is that the passions and divinations that count are those that are universal and deep.

James's ultimate criterion is the normal human mind or, more accurately, what the normal human mind finds satisfactory in the long run and on the whole. This criterion imposes real constraints on the construction of world views. No philosophy will be acceptable, for example, "which utterly denies all fundamental ground for seriousness, for effort, for hope, which says the nature of things is radically alien to human nature" (SR 89). A "sympathetic" view of the universe is thus natural or "normal." "Cynics" or "materialists" hold their positions only because "they [wrongly] think the evidence of the facts impels them" to (PU 33). Monism is also unacceptable because it reflects a "morbid mind." It appeals to us only in "moments of discouragement . . . when we are sick of self and tired of vainly striving," moments when "our own life breaks down" (Prag. 188).

Is this more than philosophical populism? I think it is. If the human mind's congruence with reality explains why our passional nature is sometimes "prophetic," superficial desires, idiosyncratic needs, and eccentric "intuitions" *should* be viewed with suspicion and, perhaps, discounted. They are not universal and deep expressions of the (normal) human mind and there is therefore no reason to trust them. (An interesting consequence is that intellectuals' intuitions should be distrusted. Many of James's critics were skeptical of the needs and believing tendencies he appealed to in arguing for the religious hypothesis, indeterminism, and meliorism. They either denied their existence [at least in their own case and in the case of other "enlightened" men and women] or thought they were pathological. James was acutely conscious of this but thought that their resistance was the result of their having stifled this side of their nature.)

Hypotheses that satisfy deep and universal needs are, then, prima facie more rational.[24] Is James abusing the concept of rationality? I submit that he is not.

The views James advocates (meliorism, indeterminism, the religious hypothesis, and even pluralism) are not adequately grounded in epistemic reason *if* epistemic reasons are restricted to what philosophers have typically regarded as such. James, however, thinks that the only *generic* concept of a good epistemic reason is the concept of the kind of consideration that, when taken into account, tends to eliminate cognitive disturbance in the long run.[25] Standard epistemic considerations[26] are likely to do so. But so are the sorts of subjective grounds James appeals to.[27] Hence, they too are good epistemic reasons.

The significance of this is not merely psychological. Taking things such as our need for significant action into account eliminates cognitive disturbance because it leads to successful adjustment to the

24. "Of two competing views of the universe which in all other respects are equal, but of which the first denies some vital human need while the second satisfies it, the second will be favored by sane men for the simple reason that it makes the world seem more rational" (*MT* 5). It is clear that James thinks this response appropriate.

25. This is strongly suggested by James's discussion in "The Sentiment of Rationality." The "sense of irrationality" is a feeling of cognitive disturbance. The "sentiment of rationality" is experienced when this disturbance has been eliminated and thought again flows smoothly. If this is right, it seems natural to identify reasons with the sorts of consideration that tend to eliminate these disturbances. *Good* reasons are considerations that tend to do so in the long run and on the whole.

26. Agreement with sense perceptions, logical coherence, congruity with our other beliefs, and so on.

27. Our reluctance to believe that reality is "foreign" or "alien," for example, or our need for significant action.

cosmos. Because this sort of success is the only criterion we *have* of being in touch with reality, the "sentiment of rationality" (the feeling we have when thought flows smoothly) is an indication that our thought has effectively engaged "the nature of things." James's sense of "good epistemic reason" and the standard sense are materially equivalent. The considerations that, when we take them into account, tend to eliminate cognitive disturbance are those which, when taken into account, put us in touch with reality. They are signs of truth and not merely utility. (We deem those views rational which yield the most "subjective satisfaction," and "if there be two conceptions, and the one seems to us, on the whole, more rational [i.e., more satisfying] than the other, we are entitled to suppose that the more rational one is the *truer* of the two" [DD 146, my emphasis]. "Our satisfactions" are "possibly really true guides to [truer beliefs about reality], not . . . guides true solely for *us*" [MT 105].)[28]

But suppose that this is James's view.[29] Is it at all plausible?

28. See *MT* 8, where James asserts that "the existence of the object, whenever the idea asserts it 'truly,' is the only reason, in innumerable cases, why the idea does work successfully." (As John E. Smith says, the qualification ["in innumerable cases"] is due to James's conviction that some future facts depend on our present responses [*Purpose and Thought*, pp. 60–61].) There is, however, an apparent inconsistency in James's thought. Although he often speaks as if truth is constituted by satisfactions, he also says that the latter are "insufficient unless reality be also incidentally led to" (*MT* 106). I believe that the inconsistency is only apparent. "Satisfaction" is sometimes used to refer to such things as emotional solace, a sense of meaning or moral significance, the release of our active powers, fulfilled expectations, coherence with our other beliefs, and so on. It is also used to refer to successful relations with reality (successful "leadings" to an idea's object or its "near neighborhood"). Satisfactions of the first kind alone are directly available to us. They therefore constitute "truth for us"; they are what truth is "known as," or are truth's "cash value." Truth for us, however, indicates that we are successfully dealing with reality and therefore possess truth simpliciter.

29. Richard Gale has objected in correspondence that it is not. (1) According to my James, "there is not a web of belief à la Quine but a web of mentation, in which is included desires and wants along with beliefs. This does not square with his conservative account of belief revision in *Pragmatism*. Do you really think that James would want to include desires, etc. in the web, since they are so totally incommensurate with empirically based beliefs. Is there a tiger in the corner? No. While I believe on the basis of visual experience that there is one there, I very much hope and desire that there is not. And since my desire is 'stronger' than my belief, I will believe that there is no tiger there! This certainly, thank God, is not James." Gales's objection seems misplaced. First, that the relevant web includes desires is clearly implied by at least one passage in *Pragmatism*. The process "by which any individual

The Reliability of Passional Reasoning

One of Gerald Myers's recent book's many virtues is its clear recognition that James believes in a "harmony between our subjective interests and the objective world;" though our "feelings and emotions . . . do not correspond exactly with the extramental world, they are clues to its nature."[30] I am not convinced, however, that Myers appreciates the *force* of James's contention.[31]

---

settles into new opinions . . . is always the same. The individual has a stock of old opinions already, but he meets a new experience that puts them to a strain. Somebody contradicts them; or in a reflective moment he discovers that they contradict each other; or he hears of facts with which they are incompatible; *or desires arise in him which they cease to satisfy.* The result is an inward trouble to which his mind till then had been a stranger, and from which he seeks to escape by modifying his previous mass of opinions" (*Prag.* 50, my emphasis). Second, the belief that there is no tiger there is clearly less satisfactory all things considered. (Believing that there is no tiger, I take no precautions and am eaten.) Therefore, it is not true (justified in the long run and on the whole). Nor am I likely to think it is, for my web of mentation also includes the *very* strong belief that, in cases like this one, wishing does not make it so. Third, as we have seen, James thinks that the desires and needs that count most heavily are those which are deep and universal. My desire that there be no tiger there may be strong and natural, but it is not as generic and deep as my desire for meaning or need for significant action. (2) Gale further complains that "a consequence of" my "account of James is that his will to believe doctrine is otiose. It seems clear," however, "that he advances it as an *alternative* to epistemic justification for belief" (my emphasis). The answer to this important objection, I think, is this. James has *two* will to believe doctrines (see footnote 12). The *weak* version of the doctrine does not rely on the claim that our instincts and needs are sometimes prophetic. The strong version does. The weak version *is* an alternative to epistemic justification. The strong version is not.

30. Myers, *James*, p. 455.

31. Myers believes that two fundamental assumptions are at work: (1) "Our subjective natures, feelings, emotions, and propensities exist as they do because something in reality harmonizes with them." (2) "Something in our feelings and experience tells us that an objective reality will fulfill our deepest yearnings." Myers thinks that the first commits James to believing that "because we want the world to be a certain way, our desire actually makes it so" and that the second rests on "the mystic's [unsupported] faith . . . in the deliverances of emotional experience" (461). This seems mistaken. James's "first premise" does not have the stated implication. Although our desires and feelings may be *signs* of what is so, they do not *make* it so (except in those special cases in which the fact that we believe in includes a "personal contribution on our part"). It would be truer to say that we have the desires and feelings we do because the world actually is "a certain way." Nor is James's "faith . . . in the deliverances of emotional experience" unsupported. As we shall see in a moment, he has (or can easily deploy) arguments for it.

The following argument lies just below the surface. (1) *Human* animals must not only adapt to their immediate environment, they
must also adapt to the "cosmos in its totality." Intelligence evolved so
that we might act successfully and enter into satisfactory relations
with the world at large. The only views that will permanently satisfy
intelligence, therefore, are those which make action possible and
meaningful and enable us to adjust satisfactorily to the world *as a
whole*. (2) The proper (normal) use of the intellectual and practical
faculties by which we construct our views is shaped by our willing
nature. Our faculties have evolved in such a way that passional factors infuse thinking. (3) Our faculties and powers have evolved as
they have because they are adaptive. (4) The best, or most natural,
explanation of the fact that these faculties and powers are adaptive is
that the beliefs they produce when properly used "correspond" (in a
rough and ready way) to reality.[32]

James's argument is open to the following objection. He assumes
that if (1) our mental capacities are the product of a long evolution,
(2) they are adaptive, and that (3) they are adaptive if and only if the
beliefs they lead to are for the most part true. He therefore concludes
that (4) on the whole, our opinions are attuned to reality. The inference from 1 to 2 is suspect. For our mental capacities may be accidental by-products of characteristics that are adaptive without our
capacities themselves being adaptive.

This criticism is effective if evolution is identified with biological (i.e., Darwinian) evolution. But James construes it more
broadly. As John E. Smith said, "The pragmatists were determined
to show the significance for philosophy of an evolutionary view-
point rooted in time."[33] For James and many other nineteenth-century intellectuals, evolution comprised psychological, social,

---

32. This line of thought is suggested by James's remarks in SR. Cf. RAT, in
which he initially says that a harmony between our faculties and the world is an article of faith (116) but goes on to argue that the fact that creatures with our faculties
have flourished implies that our "wants are to be trusted" (131). See also *VRE*
321–25, where James argues that our judgments about the value of "saintliness" are
guided by "our common sense" (321) and that these are "the fruit of an empirical
evolution" (322) that eliminates the "humanly unfit" (325). The evolutionary outlook is a constant in James's thought appearing as early as 1880. (Cf. "Remarks on
Spencer's Definition of Mind . . ." [*EP* 17–18, 19–22].)

33. Smith, *Purpose and Thought*, p. 119.

cultural, and moral development as well as biological evolution. Its aim, moreover, was adaptation to one's environment in an inclusive sense, not just (biological) survival and reproduction or the transmission of one's genes. The *human* environment is the cosmos in its totality, and the sorts of adaptation called for are psychological and moral as well as biological. If evolution is understood in this way, James's inference is more plausible. The broader evolutionary hypothesis is less firmly established, however, than the hypothesis of biological evolution.

James could also deploy two pragmatic arguments. The first is explicitly metaphysical. If the religious hypothesis is true, the world does not frustrate our deepest needs and yearnings or baffle our intellectual and practical powers. This implies that our faculties are more or less reliable. But the religious hypothesis can be pragmatically justified; that is, it can be justified by using our intellectual and practical faculties in the manner James recommends. Pragmatism's account of rationality is thus self-certifying in the sense that (unlike foundationalism) it meets its own standards; that our faculties and powers are reliable is supported by an hypothesis that can be justified by using our faculties pragmatically.

The same result can be reached more directly. Trust in the reliability of our powers is itself a basic need, a demand of human nature. Hence, other things being equal, views that affirm the trustworthiness of our faculties are more satisfactory than views that do not. Therefore, in the absence of compelling reasons for *mis*trusting them, one should believe in their reliability. Pragmatism's account of rationality is thus again self-confirming. The application of its criteria supports the claim that our powers are trustworthy.

Three Difficulties

The view I have attributed to James is clearly controversial. Three problems are especially serious.

1. The pragmatic justifications of the reliability of our faculties are ultimately circular. That, in itself, is hardly surprising. Justifications of the reliability of sense perception, or of deductive and inductive

reasoning, typically rely on claims established by using these procedures. Circles of this kind are inescapable.

Are the self-certifying practices that James recommends subject to
special difficulties? They may be, but what are they? Certainly not
that the practices *countenance* inconsistency, obliviousness to obvious
facts, wishful thinking, and rampant subjectivism, for they provide
safeguards against these errors. Is the problem that different people
can employ these methods and arrive at different and inconsistent
conclusions? No doubt they can. But this objection, too, has little
force as a similar complaint can be directed against *any* account of
the type of reasoning involved in philosophy, literary and artistic
criticism, and moral or political reflection. It is true that proponents
of other methods often *assure* us that their proper use will resolve disagreement, but so does James.[34] Are the promises made by advocates
of more familiar procedures more reassuring or better grounded? I,
for one, doubt it. It is nevertheless true that pragmatic reasoning's validity is controversial in a way in which that of standard forms of reasoning is not. It is also true that the pragmatic justifications of
pragmatic reasoning offered in the preceding section will only convince those already persuaded of its legitimacy. These worries are legitimate and will be addressed in Chapter 4.

2. James is acutely conscious of the role psychological factors play
in reasoning. I do not think that he is sufficiently sensitive to the ways
in which cultural and social structures shape our psychological
processes or sufficiently attentive to the ways in which projection, re-
pression, false consciousness, and so on distort reasoning. Although
James does not totally ignore culture, he clearly believes that individual psychology is basic. The explanatory line runs from the psyche to
culture—not the other way around. Even if James is right about this
(and I think he is), culture's importance is not adequately recognized.
Furthermore, even though he insists on the importance of the un-
conscious and of the study of abnormal psychology, he never seri-

34. *Pragmatism* and other late works clearly evince James's belief that the pragmatic method can do a better job of resolving outstanding metaphysical disputes. In
VRE, James expresses the hope that the "science of religions" can "help to bring
about consensus of opinion" on (at least some) religious issues (446).

ously considers the possibility that false consciousness might be pervasive. For example, is James's picture of human nature (which stresses
humanity's horror of meaninglessness and need for significant action)
a disguised portrait of himself? Or a portrait of a cultivated American
in the latter part of the nineteenth century? Is it, in other words, a
projection of his own hopes and fears, or the hopes and fears of his
social class? Not entirely, surely, but perhaps in part.

What is needed, I think, is a "critique of passional reason"—a
convincing account of the conditions under which our passional nature may, and may not, legitimately affect the construction and assessment of beliefs and arguments. An account of this kind should
incorporate the insights of Freud, Marx, and Foucault, among others, and of theologians such as Calvin who have examined the ways
in which human perversity distorts reasoning. The epistemologies of
Newman and (especially) Edwards may be superior to the epistemology of James in this respect because of their acute sensitivity to the
epistemic effects of sin.[35] (More on this in Chapter 6.)

3. James's account of rationality rests on the assumption that
human beings share common needs and interests. If they do not, appeals to our passional nature can only lead to relativism. Nor will
there be much reason to trust its promptings. Why should we think
that our passions and feelings are clues to reality if they are not shared
by others and are simply quirks of our own psyche or reflections of
our own social circumstances?

Postmodernists deny the existence of a common human nature.[36]
They overstate their case, but concepts of human nature *are* problematic. They are only too often portraits of their authors or of a
specific class, culture, or gender.

To make matters worse, James himself often talks as if we *do not*
have the same needs or share the same fundamental interests. Minds

35. If James is right, however, a belief in the religious hypothesis or indeterminism or meliorism is *not* an expression of false consciousness. James thinks that the
discovery of the passional roots and of the history of these beliefs does not delegiti-
matize them.

36. Although postmodernists differ, they tend to agree that all but a few basic biological needs are culturally created. Even these are shaped by systems of power, ide-
ology, and so on.

such as Spinoza's, for example, have a "passion for simplification," whereas minds such as Hume's have a "passion for distinguishing" (SR 66). "Men's active impulses are [also] so differently mixed that a philosophy fit in this respect for Bismark will almost certainly be unfit for a valetudinarian poet" (SR 88). The analogies we use to unlock the universe are "at bottom accidents more or less of personal vision" (PU 10). In the last analysis, *temperament* "loads the evidence . . . one way or the other, making for a more sentimental or a more hard-hearted view of the universe" (*Prag.* 19).

There clearly is a tension between this important strand in James's thought and his appeal to generic needs and interests. Whether he *contradicts* himself is less certain.

James seems to think that what varies are not basic needs and interests as such but their relative strength. Furthermore, clashes of temperament only become *acute* when one need or interest dominates others. But cases of this kind are atypical, for "most of us . . . are a mixture of opposite ingredients, each one present very moderately" (*Prag.* 20). Because the final court of appeal is "the *normal* run of minds" (*Prag.* 36, my emphasis), irreconcilable clashes of "temperament" are irrelevant (or least not decisive).

Each "partial system" may also be *true* as far as it goes. "The divine," for example, "can mean no single quality" but "a group of qualities, by being champions of which in alternation, different men may all find worthy missions. Each attitude being a syllable in human nature's total message, it takes the whole of us to spell the meaning out completely" (*VRE* 477).[37] (James's point, I take it, is that there is likely to be partial truth even in idiosyncratic visions when these are recurrent, persistent, deep, and fairly successful in enabling their advocates to cope with reality.) Finally, James believes that our differences will largely sort themselves out in the course of humanity's evolution. Judgments of credibility reflect our needs and ideals, and these are "the fruit of an empirical evolution" that eventually weeds out the "humanly unfit" (*VRE* 321, 325).

These considerations probably are not sufficient to defuse the objection. Whether the generic needs, interests, and sentiments James

---

37. Some of these partial systems, however, may be "wider and completer" than others (*VRE* 478, n.).

appeals to are real, and *sufficiently determinate* to do the work he wants them to, remains doubtful. I suspect there is no useful common denominator. We *can* abstract common features (e.g., a need for meaning), but these will be too thin to be of much help. There are, however, significant family resemblances. It is at least possible that these will be sufficient to make the Jamesian project feasible.

James's approach has both a disadvantage and an advantage. Appeals to generic human needs, interests, and sentiments can at best only establish James's generic religious hypotheses. More robust convictions must be justified by reasoning processes that are infused by affections that are not universally shared (true benevolence, for example).

The advantage of James's approach, on the other hand, is its avoidance of relativism. If the needs, interests, and sentiments it appeals to are universal, as James thinks, their effect on reasoning will not significantly vary from one individual or culture to another. The credentials of invariant features of human cognitive processes (reliance on perception, for example, or the use of induction) can be questioned by skeptics, but they are not subject to real (as distinguished from philosophical) doubt. True benevolence, however, and the moral and spiritual virtues that Newman appeals to, are not universally—or perhaps even widely—shared. Whether Edwards's and Newman's positions lead to relativism will be discussed in Chapter 5.

[4]

Subjectivism and Circularity

This chapter addresses two objections to which we have often alluded in earlier chapters. (1) One is epistemically justified in believing *p* if and only if one's circumstances (including one's reasons if any) entitle one to think *p* true. Epistemic justification should be distinguished from pragmatic or prudential or moral justification because one can be justified in believing that it would be useful or prudent or good to believe *p* without being entitled to think *p* true. The views examined in Chapters 1, 2, and 3 confuse the two. "Reasons of the heart" have a bearing on pragmatic or prudential or moral justification; they have no bearing on epistemic justification. Views such as Edwards's, Newman's, or James's are open invitations to wishful thinking, prejudice, and other forms of irrational believing.

(2) Nor can their positions be defended without circularity. Edwards's and Newman's accounts of rational believing are unlikely to persuade those who are not already convinced of theism and thus (according to these theories) have the moral and spiritual dispositions whose epistemic credentials are in question. James's defense of the rationality of religious belief (or belief in indeterminism or meliorism) is unlikely to convince those who are not already prepared to trust the promptings of their passional nature.

Both of these objections are serious. Both can be met.

Subjectivism

That passional factors *should* affect reasoning strikes most philosophers as epistemically, or even morally, objectionable. Louis Pojman's *Religious Belief and the Will* is a forceful expression of this view.[1] Because his objections are representative, I shall focus on several of the most important. I will show that they rest on a common assumption—that our passional nature is not a reliable guide to objective truth. As Edwards, Newman, and James deny this, these objections beg the question.

Let me begin with two preliminary comments. First, people such as Edwards are not recommending that we cultivate certain beliefs by viewing the evidence selectively. Edwards is not advising us to *ignore* any relevant evidence but, instead, to view *all* of the evidence (assess its force) in a certain way. Second, although the truly benevolent are not impartial in the sense of not allowing their passions to affect their judgment, they may exhibit other intellectual virtues closely associated with impartiality. Even though a truly benevolent person, "let[s] his wants . . . [or other passional factors] enter into the judgment he makes" (199) by allowing them to affect his evaluations of the evidence's overall force, he can "seek out evidence and pay attention to criticism and counter claims, . . . support his judgment with recognizable good reasons," "be open to the possibility that he might be wrong," and "revise and reject his belief in the light of new information" (198, 203). It does not follow, for example, that the truly benevolent who believe that they are in an epistemically superior position can safely ignore criticisms made by nontheists on the ground that the latter are in an epistemically inferior position with respect to the evaluation of arguments to theological conclusions. For the theory does not imply that theists have a monopoly on logical acumen, that they will not sometimes fail to notice relevant points or draw relevant distinctions, or that they cannot have their own blind spots.

---

1. Louis Pojman, *Religious Belief and the Will* (London: Routledge and Kegan Paul, 1986). All page references in this section are to Pojman's book unless otherwise noted. I shall use a certain freedom in interpreting his arguments as my primary target is not Pojman but the view he represents.

Nevertheless, the truly benevolent *do* allow their judgments to be influenced by their new wants and interests. Whether this sort of bias or partiality is undesirable is another matter. Consider four arguments that purport to show that it is.

1. Pojman borrows one argument from Richard Gale.[2] "To be an autonomous person is to have a high degree of warranted beliefs at one's disposal upon which to base one's actions. There is a tendency to lower one's freedom of choice as one lowers the repertoire of [evidentially] well-justified beliefs regarding a plan of action." Allowing one's beliefs to be determined by passional factors is also "a sort of lying [to oneself] or cheating [oneself] in that it enjoins believing against what has the best guarantee of being the truth." "Cognitive-voliting,"[3] then, "decreases one's own freedom and personhood." "Since . . . it is wrong to lessen one's autonomy or personhood, it is wrong to lessen the degree of [evidential] justification of one's beliefs on important matters" (188–89).

Several things are wrong with this argument. Cognitive-voliting does not involve lying to oneself if one does not deceive oneself about the real force of the evidence. James, for example, often appears to take the same view of the evidence's force as his critics. He allows passional factors to determine beliefs that he too thinks are not evidentially justified. It is difficult to see how this involves self-deception unless "seeing that the evidence for *p* is insufficient" entails "not believing that *p* is true"—an entailment James would deny.[4]

2. Richard Gale, "William James and the Ethics of Belief," *American Philosophical Quarterly* 17 (1980), 1–14.

3. Pojman uses this term "to signify 'directly obtaining a belief by willing to have it' " (viii). I will use it more broadly to signify "(knowingly) allowing one's beliefs to be influenced by passional factors."

4. James talks this way in "The Will to Believe" (in *The Will to Believe and Other Essays in Popular Philosophy* [New York, c. 1896; reprint, New York: Dover, 1956]) and elsewhere, but on other occasions expresses a view more like Edwards's. Our passional nature affects our assessment of the *force* of the evidence. (See Chapter 3.) The explanation for this apparent inconsistency, I believe, is this: James identifies the evidence's "objective" force with the force attributed to it by disinterested (or even hostile?) inquirers and not with what he regards as its *real* force. If I am right, then (contrary to standard interpretations) James's "volitional believing" does sometimes express what seems to one to be the evidence's real force.

Even if the entailment holds, it is difficult to see why a person necessarily deceives herself when she consciously allows passional factors to affect her assessment of an argument's real strength. We could, of course, *identify* the evidence's real force with the force it seems to have when we abstract from the influence of subjective qualities such as hope, faith, true benevolence, and other holy dispositions. But to do so begs the question.

Nor is it clear that "Being an autonomous person involves having a high degree of warranted beliefs at one's disposal" is more plausible than "Being an autonomous person involves having a high degree of *true* beliefs at one's disposal." Consider two people A and B. A has a high degree of warranted but false beliefs. B has a high degree of true but insufficiently warranted beliefs. Is it obvious that A is more autonomous? Only if autonomy is (largely) *defined* in terms of rational belief formation. Is acting on the basis of one's passional nature heteronomous, that is, constrained by something external to the self? It is *if* (as Kant thought) reason is one's real self. But Edwards, Newman, and James believe that it is not. In *their* view, our heart or passional nature is the deepest thing about us. Nor is it obvious that B's freedom of choice is less. (Both B and A can be contracausally free, and B is, after all, in a better position to satisfy his desires.) The underlying assumption, of course, is that beliefs that are determined by "impartial" assessments of relevant evidence are more likely to be true. That this holds of *all* subject matters, however, is precisely what is at issue. James and Edwards, for example, think it does not when the propositions at stake are "generic" hypotheses about the metaphysical shape of reality (James) or statements about God and our relation to Him (Edwards).

2. Another argument derives from William Clifford. "General truthfulness is a desideratum without which society cannot function" (189). Unwarranted beliefs that do not directly injure ourselves or others may do so indirectly. "Beliefs do not exist in isolation from each other, so that to overthrow one belief may have reverberations throughout our entire noetic structure, affecting many of our beliefs. . . . Cognitive-voliting, as Bernard Williams has pointed out" may be the sort of project that " 'tends in the end to involve total destruction

of the world of reality, to lead to paranoia.' " It injures society as well because it impairs the habit of truth seeking that "if it is to be effective at all, . . . must be deeply engrained within us"(190).[5]

There are also problems with *this* argument. In the first place, it is not obvious that people's beliefs are that tightly connected. It is significant, I think, that Pascal, Kierkegaard, and James were probably *less* credulous with respect to most matters than others. (All three had deeply skeptical temperaments.) Nor were Edwards and Newman more credulous with respect to nonreligious matters than their educated contemporaries. It is also difficult to see how a Jamesian will to believe (as usually interpreted) could impair one's evidence-evaluating faculties when one of its *presuppositions* is a clear view of what James *and* his critics *agree* is the evidence's "objective" strength (that it does not clearly point to a belief or to its denial).[6] As for Edwards and Newman, we may concede that willfully believing that the evidence has a force it lacks can impair our evidence-evaluating faculties. Identifying the evidence's real strength with the force it has in the eyes of the "impartial," however, begs the question.

Pojman's second argument, of course, rests on the same assumption as his first—that beliefs determined by passional factors are less likely to be true. Why should we believe this?

3. The third argument runs, "The very concept of having a belief entails the belief that if the belief is true, there must be some connection between it and states of affairs in the world" (172). In other words, "belief that *p* seems to imply the thought of a causal chain stretching back from the belief to a primary relationship with the world and so faithfully representing the world" (175). Allowing one's beliefs to be determined by passional factors severs this connection. "It is a confusion to believe that any given belief is true simply on the basis of being willed. As soon as the believer discovers the basis

5. The internal quote is from Bernard Williams, "Deciding to Believe," in *Problems of the Self* (Cambridge, England: Cambridge University Press, 1972).

6. James's official position is that "cognitive-voliting" is in order only when an issue is "intellectually undecidable" i.e., when the "so-called objective evidence" is (by commonly agreed standards) inconclusive.

of his belief—as being caused by the will alone—he must drop the belief" (172). Beliefs arising from passional factors are like beliefs based on imagination. When we discover their origins, we discard them as worthless.

Several things need sorting out. It is certainly true that except for a few cases in which the future depends on our current attitudes, "wishing does not make it so" (171). Neither does wanting, needing, willing, nor feeling. Beliefs are made true by the states of affairs they represent and not by the wishes, wants, feelings, and volitions of the people who have them.[7] But neither Edwards nor James, for example, would deny this. Nor would they deny the existence of some sort of causal link between true beliefs and the world they faithfully represent. What, then, is their position? Although a need for meaning, a desire for significant action, or holy dispositions do not *make* the beliefs they (partly) determine true, they are *correlated* with states of affairs that do. For these needs, desires, and feelings are causally connected (in the right way) with the way the world is. James, for example, thinks that our "willing nature" has evolved as it has because following its dictates has enabled us to adjust more successfully to reality. Behavior based on our passional nature would not be so successful if it led us to misrepresent egregiously things as they are. Similarly, Edwards's *The Nature of True Virtue* attempts to show that the "mechanism" underlying the new sense of heart, that is, true benevolence, "agrees" with reality. Reality's core is an infinite benevolence—the world's only true substance and its only true cause. The benevolence of the saints is grounded in this and mirrors it. Edwards concludes that benevolence is not "arbitrary" but agrees "with the necessary nature of things" (*TV* 620). Assuming that cognitive voliting invariably severs the connection between beliefs and the states of affairs they represent begs the question against views like these.

4. The best argument against cognitive-voliting is inductive. Extensive experience has shown that need, desire, and other passional factors can adversely affect judgment. It has also shown that method-

---

7. To place this in perspective, however, we should remember that cognitions and perceptions do not make beliefs true either.

ical efforts to reduce their influence can serve the cause of truth. Science is the most impressive example.

This argument, however, is also inconclusive. Edwards would agree with James. "Almost always" in science, "and even in human affairs in general," we should "save ourselves from any chance of believing falsehood, by not making up our minds at all till objective evidence has come" (WTB 20). They would agree, in other words, that passional considerations are out of order in most cases *like those in the sample.*[8] Both would deny that we can legitimately extrapolate from these cases to others with different subject matters (the metaphysical and moral structure of reality, for example, or things of the spirit). As we have just seen, they have arguments purporting to show that with these subject matters some passional factors *are* reliable guides to truth. Simply to assume that the generalization concerning the adverse effects of passional factors can be extended to areas like these begs the question.

It may not, for example, apply to ethics. Aristotle argues that moral reasoning goes astray when it is not informed by a correct understanding of the good life. The latter, however, depends on properly cultivated dispositions as well as sound reasoning. If one's emotional temper is defective or has been perverted by corrupt education, one cannot appreciate the good. As a result, one misconstrues the nature of the good life, and one's practical deliberations miscarry. Now according to classical theism, God is the good. One would therefore expect a properly cultivated heart to be a necessary condition of grasping truths about Him.[9]

If theism is true, and if it is also true that subjective qualifications would be needed to know God if God existed,[10] there is reason to

8. The qualification ("most") is designed to accommodate cases in which there may be special reasons for overriding our prima facie duty to exclude "subjective" factors in science and everyday life—cases, for example, in which we have moral obligations to trust others.

9. If God is not the good but "only" a perfect instance of it (or its supreme exemplar), this argument is less compelling. The fact remains that dispassion and disinterest are sometimes epistemically harmful.

10. On the latter, see C. Stephen Evans, "Kierkegaard and Plantinga on Belief in God: Subjectivity as the Ground of Properly Basic Religious Beliefs," *Faith and Philosophy* 5 (1988), 25–39. Cf. Edwards who argues that if there were a divine glory distinguishing the Gospel from merely human books, sin "would blind men from discerning" it (RA 301). "It is not rational to suppose, if there be any such

think that cognitive-voliting is sometimes reliable. In refusing to allow our passional nature to affect our judgment on religious matters, we may therefore be prejudging the case against people like Edwards. Indeed, we may be unwittingly assuming that theism is highly improbable or that it is unlikely that subjective qualifications would be needed to know God if theism were true. For suppose that John is reluctant to trust his passional nature but that the evidence suggests to him that theism has a significant chance of being correct—.3, for example, or even .5. Suppose he also has good, although not conclusive, reasons for thinking that if theism is true, refusing to trust his passional nature is likely to permanently debar him from acquiring a vitally important truth. Suppose finally (as seems plausible)[11] that it is more important for us to believe theism if theism is true than to believe it false if it is false. Is it unreasonable for John to trust his passional nature in these circumstances? It is difficult to believe that it is.[12]

The arguments examined in this section seem, then, to beg the question by implicitly assuming that theism is false or that subjective qualifications are not needed to know God. Still, theists such as Edwards and James may be no better off. For attempts to show that our passional nature is sometimes reliable may also beg the question; arguments like theirs are not likely to persuade those who suppress the promptings of their hearts or refuse to be guided by them. A fully adequate defense of positions like Edwards's must therefore show that they are not vitiated by circularity. We shall turn to this question in the next section.

Circularity

Edwards's arguments for the objectivity of the saints' new use of their noetic faculties are based on scripture and theistic metaphysics. James's arguments rest on his psychology, his pragmatism, and (what

---

excellency in divine things, that wicked men should see it" since the power of their "filthy lusts" prevents them from "relishing" it (DSL 16).

11. Cf. Richard Swinburne, *Faith and Reason* (Oxford: Clarendon, 1981), p. 81

12. There may be even less reason to think that I should not engage in cognitive-voliting to *strengthen* my belief in God when the evidence seems to me to make it (even slightly) more probable than not.

he believes to be) the facts of evolution. The premises of these arguments do not merely restate their conclusions, or immediately entail them in the trivial way a conjunction entails its conjuncts or "Some S is P" entails its converse. Are they circular in some less obvious way? For the sake of simplicity, I will focus on Edwards.

In examining the question of circularity, it will be helpful to distinguish three things: (1) the conclusion that true benevolence and other holy dispositions are needed to use one's epistemic faculties rightly, (2) an implication of this conclusion, namely, that sincere theists are in a superior epistemic position with respect to rational arguments about "divine things," and (3) the theist's reliance on his or her own assessments of the evidence's force.

I shall argue that the *conclusion* is not presupposed. But theists do rely on their own assessments of the evidence's force, and this commits them to thinking that they are in a superior epistemic position with respect to its evaluation. I shall also argue, however, that *any* reliance on one's own assessments in matters of basic dispute involves similar assumptions. The kind of circularity that infects positions like Edwards's affects all areas in which there are deep disagreements about the overall force of complicated bodies of evidence.

Let us begin by asking three questions raised by William Alston in another context.[13] Are theists such as Edwards implicitly assuming the truth of their conclusion? Could they be convinced of the truth of their premises (i.e., of the propositions of theistic metaphysics that support it) if they doubted the conclusion or denied it? Must they appeal to the conclusion to justify retaining their confidence of the truth of the premises in the face of their critics' objections?

Are theists who employ premises that imply that true benevolence or other holy dispositions are epistemically necessary implicitly assuming the truth of the conclusion? Not clearly. Not only may the conclusion not previously have occurred to them; they also may initially (before they see where their premises are leading them) share the standard conception of rationality and simply accuse their critics of failing to appreciate the force of a body of evidence (the

13. William Alston, "Epistemic Circularity," *Philosophy and Phenomenological Research* 47 (1986), 1–30.

evidence for their brand of theism) that should convince anyone who employs normal epistemic procedures of the truth of their premises.

Could these theists be convinced of the truth of their premises if they doubted or denied the conclusion? For the reasons just given, I do not see why not. The evidence for premises such as "An omnipotent benevolence is the only true substance and the only true cause" does not include the epistemic theory in question, and (as we have just seen) they initially share their critics' conception of rationality. But, of course, the challenge has not yet been pushed far enough.

What is primarily at issue is not the premises' support for the argument's conclusion. Edwards's theistic metaphysics entails his epistemic theory or makes it probable. What is at issue are the premises themselves, the theistic metaphysics in which the controversial epistemic theory is embedded. The theists' critics doubt or deny that the evidence for the metaphysics is sufficient to support it. Theists such as Edwards believe that it is.

But in trusting their own assessments of the evidence, are not theists of this sort implicitly assuming that their judgments and those of others who make similar assessments are reliable while their critics' assessments are not? And if they are, and have their wits about them, can they help noticing that those who make assessments like theirs are theists while most of those who do not are not? Are they not, then, implicitly assuming that theists are, by and large, better judges of the evidence for theological conclusions; that is, that they are somehow in a superior epistemic position with respect to it? Are they not, in other words, implicitly assuming the truth of one of their conclusion's more controversial implications? If, as seems likely, the answer is "Yes," we have uncovered our circle.

What is not clear, however, is that this kind of circularity is vicious or should undermine the theist's confidence in her conclusion. For she *has* evidence that supports it and believes her conclusion because of it. (It is important to remember that the special perspective on the evidence furnished by her new holy dispositions is not functioning as a premise or an inference rule in her argument, nor is it part of her evidence for her premises.)

Furthermore, she may *be* justified in trusting her assessment of the evidence's force (since, if the theory is true,[14] she is making it in the right way), even though (1) she has not *justified* her confidence and will not be in a position to do so until she has drawn her conclusion, and even though (2) she *cannot* justify every premise, inference rule, *and epistemic attitude or posture* involved in arriving at it without falling into a logical circle.[15] (Her justification would be logically circular since she would have to appeal to her conclusion to justify her special slant on the evidence.)

A point by Michael Smith is also relevant.[16] Arguments whose conclusions appear among their premises are obviously circular. A more subtle kind of circularity occurs when principles of reasoning are supported by arguments that employ them. The circularity we have uncovered is a bit like the latter. (Assessing the force of certain sorts of evidence from the perspective of true benevolence bears some resemblance to using a principle of reason. Neither appears among the premises. Both are employed in deriving the conclusion.) Smith contends that arguments of the second type sometimes have explanatory value. (Edwards's theistic metaphysics, for example, explains why the truly benevolent are better judges of the relevant evidence.) Although arguments of this kind cannot provide "original justification," they can make principles of reason and epistemic attitudes more reasonable than they would otherwise be; for the existence of a plausible explanation of an alleged fact can add to its probability.[17]

The important point, however, is this. The type of circularity we have uncovered infects history, archeology, paleontology, philosophy, literary and artistic criticism, and every other discipline in which apparently competent inquirers disagree about the overall force of complicated bodies of evidence. Philosophers or historians, for example, who think they have good arguments must implicitly assume

14. And we cannot assume it is false without begging the question.
15. This sentence relies heavily on Alston.
16. Michael Smith, "Virtuous Circles," *Southern Journal of Philosophy* 25 (1987), 207–20.
17. For this consideration to carry any weight with the theist's critics, they must concede that (1) there is some nonnegligible chance that the alleged fact obtains and that (2) the explanation has *some* plausibility. (Although they need not concede that the fact *does* obtain or that the explanation is plausible *überhaupt*.)

that their assessments of the evidence's force are more reliable than those of their critics. They must therefore assume that the judgments of others who typically assess evidence of that kind as they do are more reliable than the judgments of those who assess it differently. But this implies that those who assess evidence of that sort as they do are in a superior epistemic position with respect to it.

And is this not, indeed, being tacitly presupposed? As Newman and others have pointed out, complicated assessments of historical and philosophical hypotheses (for instance) not only reflect a person's intelligence, education, and information; they also reflect that person's experience in dealing with issues of that kind, his or her imagination or lack of it, sensitivity to certain kinds of evidence, temperament, values, and a host of other tacit factors. If a good philosopher or historian is challenged to justify a controversial assessment of the evidence's overall force, does she not ultimately have to appeal to her critics' alleged blindness to the importance of certain kinds of evidence, their failures of imagination, deficiencies in their experience, or something else of the sort?[18] And yet she surely knows that her critics would deny that things such as these are distorting their judgment. Can she sustain her charge against her critics without begging the question by arguing that their blindness to their deficiencies is itself partly caused by them? (One of the effects of self-deception, for example, is to conceal the fact that one is suffering from it. The same is true of a lack of aesthetic taste or moral sensitivity, and of other defects of the same kind.) I, for one, doubt it.

But *are* the epistemic situations of the truly benevolent, on the one hand, and historians, philosophers, and so on, on the other, really parallel? Consider the following objection of William Rowe:[19]

> The circle involved in the theist's reasoning to the conclusion that special divine gifts are (i) given only to theists, and (ii) are needed to use one's epistemic faculties rightly . . . probably . . . isn't a bad circle. The conclusion does imply that sincere theists are in a superior epistemic position with respect to rational arguments about "divine things." But if all the theist does is hold that she

18. Appeals of this sort are usually implicit, of course.
19. In correspondence.

(and other theists) are right in accepting the argument, while nontheists who reject it are wrong, then that sort of circle (if it should be called a circle at all) also holds for philosophers who are incompatibilists accepting an argument for incompatibilism, and holding that they are right to accept its premises, while also holding that compatibilists are wrong in rejecting the premises or in rejecting the inference to its conclusion. But there is the potential for a bad circle in the theist's argument. For if the theist goes on to *explain* the nontheist's rejection of the argument for the theist's special access, as well as to explain the theist's acceptance of the argument for the theist's special access, by appealing to the conclusion of that argument, the theist implicitly assumes the truth of the conclusion in explaining why its premises are regarded as truth-conducive by the theist and less than truth-conducive by the nontheist. And in giving this explanation the theist is implying that the premises are likely true by virtue of being assented to by those who are epistemically superior to those who dissent from the premises. In short, the theist is using the conclusion of the argument to show that the premises are likely true. I don't see a similar kind of circle in the debate between compatibilists and incompatibilists.

I have three things to say about this objection. In the first place, this way of putting the objection suggests that the theist's slant on the evidence is *part* of it, or is one of her *reasons* for accepting the premises. And this is false. Compare this case with another. An honest, critical, and fairminded evolutionary biologist's *take* on her evidence is not *part* of her evidence. Nor are her honesty, fairmindedness, and so on among her *reasons* for her belief, although the presence of these excellences helps *explain* why she holds the belief she does and not that of some less scrupulous or more credulous colleague.

In the second place, similar circles *can* arise in debates between compatibilists and incompatibilists. Incompatibilists believe that determinism precludes moral responsibility. My actions are free only if I possess a capacity (in some suitably robust sense) to act otherwise. If my choices are determined by causes beyond my control, I do not. Compatibilists, of course, disagree and the matter is often left at that point. But a reflective incompatibilist will undoubtedly won-der why her intuitions and those of her opponent differ.[20] Suppose she explains the compatibilist's failure to see what she sees by his overattention to the analogies between human and animal behavior and to routine human activity, and his insensitivity to the peculiarities of human moral behavior, especially in what James called the "the lonely emergencies of life" (SR 105)—by the absence, in other words, of the epistemic attitudes and postures that have led *her* to read the evidence rightly. If the compatibilist rejects this account of his intuitions (as he undoubtedly will), is not the incompatibilist likely to explain the compatibilist's rejection of her explanation by citing *the same defects*? And if her original explanation is *correct*, is she not *right* to do so? For the misdirected attention and insensitivity the incompatibilist alludes to will (if genuine) make it difficult for the compatibilist to recognize his own blindness.[21]

There is, of course, this difference between the incompatibilist's position and the theist's. The incompatibilist is not using the *conclusion* of her original argument (that determinism is incompatible with moral responsibility) to explain her opponent's blindness. The theist is. Nonetheless, the cases are relevantly similar. For in drawing her conclusion, the incompatibilist contextually implies that *her* take on the evidence (and therefore the take of those who assess evidence of that sort as she does) is epistemically superior to the compatibilist's take on the evidence. The *act* of drawing her conclusion about determinism and human responsibility thus *contextually implies* something very much like the conclusion of Edwards's (or Newman's or James's) argument. Furthermore, the same intuitions, hunches, pro-

20. Thinking that one's assessment of the evidence is right and one's critic's assessment wrong does not *logically* commit one to a particular explanation of the disagreement, or even to the *existence* of an explanation. But it may *rationally* do so. We are uncomfortable when we cannot explain the nature of the error committed by opponents who seem to be (and in many ways are) our intellectual peers. (They are as intelligent, highly trained, informed, and fair-minded as we are.) Our discomfort is rational. For without an explanation, it is not clear that we are *entitled* to think that our assessment of the evidence is correct whereas theirs is not.

21. It may be possible in some cases to explain an opponent's resistance to an argument purporting to show that some defect places him in an inferior epistemic position without appealing to that defect. But (in the interesting cases at least) the explanation will typically be provided by the defect that the conclusion of the disputed argument attributes to him.

clivities, values, attentions, and sensitivities that determine the incompatibilist's take on her evidence are also likely to figure in her explanation of the compatibilist's blindness and of his resistence to her
explanation of his blindness. (His attention is misdirected, for example, or he is insensitive to evidence to which she is sensitive.)

My third point is this. There is a bad circle *if* the theist appeals to
her possession of true benevolence or some other holy disposition to
justify her acceptance of arguments for the conclusion that the possession of these dispositions places one in an epistemically superior position with respect to the evaluation of arguments to theological
conclusions and her rejection of arguments to the contrary. For in
that case she implicitly appeals to the conclusion whose truth is in dispute.[22] It does not follow, however, that the theist is involved in a bad
circle if she only appeals to her holy dispositions and her opponent's
lack of them to *explain* why she accepts arguments to the conclusion
that these dispositions provide special access to the evaluation of the
force of arguments to theological conclusions while her critics reject
them. For one can (correctly) explain one's own or another's conduct
without either justifying it or showing it to be unjustified. Suppose,
for example, that a psychoanalytic theory incorporates a psychoanalytic explanation of why its opponents reject it. Suppose in particular
that the theory implies that their rejection is an expression of unresolved Oedipal conflicts. It is question-begging to appeal to this explanation to show that opponents of the theory are unjustified in
rejecting it and the explanation of resistance that it incorporates. For
the truth of the theory and the explanation it includes is precisely
what is at issue. The fact that those who resist the theory reject the
explanation of their resistance does not show that the explanation is
incorrect, however. Nor does it show it to be circular. That Jones re-
sists the diagnosis of his resistance as the expression of unresolved
Oedipal conflicts, because of unresolved Oedipal conflicts does not
explain his resistance in terms of itself. The explicandum is not part
of the explicans. I conclude, then, that Rowe's objection can be met.

If my remarks in this section are on target, then the kind of circularity that infects arguments like Edwards's also infects reasoning in

22. I.e., she implicitly assumes that (e.g.) true benevolence is needed properly to
assess the force of arguments to theological conclusions.

other disciplines, including philosophy and history.[23] Should one therefore conclude that one is not entitled to say that one knows, or is rationally confident of, propositions in contested areas like these? That one is not entitled, for example confidently to believe in the truth of physicalism, incompatibilism, or anything else disputed by one's peers? Few philosophers would say, "Yes." If they would not, they are not in a position to cast the first stone.

That the type of circularity that infects accounts like Edwards's is endemic to most disciplines, including philosophy, implies that the critic's only recourse is to provide *special* reasons for thinking that the theist's slant on the evidence is unreliable while his own is not. He must explain, for example, why true benevolence and other holy dispositions (Edwards) or a need for meaning and significant action (James) are likely to prove deceptive while inhibiting their influence is not. As we saw in the first section of this chapter, it will be difficult for the critic to do this without begging the question.

Neither side can avoid circularity. This is disturbing *if* a non-question-begging way of mutually resolving basic disagreements over the overall force of a body of evidence is a necessary condition of the possibility of being rational in these matters. If it is, theists are not the only ones in deep trouble.

The objections we have considered in this chapter thus seem inconclusive. But we are not out of the woods yet. For views like Edwards's can also be found in other traditions.[24] Consider the claim that the best evidence for the authority of the *Vedas* is their intrinsic luminosity. Or the Buddhist doctrine of skillful means that implies that one's ability to understand spiritual truths depends on one's spiritual maturity or lack of it. Nor are positions of this kind found only in religious traditions. James's account of our passional nature is an example. The problem, of course, is that these positions are used to justify very different assessments of the same evidence. Does the position I am defending commit us to relativism? We will discuss this question in the next chapter.

23. Does it infect all disciplines? Probably not mathematics and logic. But it infects reasoning in the social sciences and humanities. It also infects reasoning in the hard sciences. Evolutionary biology and cosmology are good examples.

24. Or can easily be constructed from them.

[5]

The Specter of Relativism

Christians and other sincere theists typically contend that their new dispositions and feelings place them in a superior epistemic position with respect to certain questions. Advaitins, Buddhists, and other nontheists make similar claims. So too do historians, philosophers, critics, and others who are confident of opinions established by informal reasoning in matters of fundamental dispute. (See Chapter 4, second section.) There appear to be no neutral criteria that can be used successfully to adjudicate these conflicting claims to epistemic superiority. Does the view that I am defending, then, implicitly commit us to relativism? We can best address the question by examining the more general problem of which it is a part: the apparently relativistic implications of fundamental disagreements over basic standards of rationality.

Disagreement and the Plausibility of Relativism

Why should agreement or disagreement even be thought to be relevant to the question of cognitive relativism? That standards of rationality and criteria of truth vary does not *entail* that there are no objectively valid standards of rationality or that truth itself is not objective. Nor would the nonexistence of objective truth or objectively valid standards of rationality entail that human beings would not share the same standards and accept the same criteria.[1] So why do disputes over the existence of shared standards and criteria play such a large role in debates between cognitive relativists and their opponents? That they do is undeniable. As Patrick Gardiner has pointed out,[2] modern relativism has two principal roots: Kant's Copernican revolution that insists on the human contribution to knowledge, and Herder's recognition of the "irreducibility" of cultures and the diversity of a human nature that is formed and shaped by those cultures.

It is easy to explain why diversity should *seem* important.

1. A recognition of the variety of cultures and intellectual systems is not new. What is new is a widely diffused appreciation of their depth and richness. A widespread appreciation of Islam or Buddhism for example, or a sympathetic grasp of what it is like to be an intelligent and sensitive Muslim or Buddhist, is a recent phenomenon in Western history. Now people's confidence in their opinions and assumptions is often shaken when they find informed, sensitive, and intelligent men and women who fail to share them. Their doubts are likely to deepen when they find that their intellectual adversaries are not convinced by the arguments they introduce to establish the superiority of their own insights. In these circumstances, a pervasive though not always fully articulated doubt concerning the objective validity of one's fundamental assumptions and habitual ways of thinking is not surprising.

2. An unrestricted cognitive relativism is perhaps more widely diffused in the modern West than in any previous culture. Even so, it remains a minority position. Although often espoused by intellectuals in the humanities and social sciences, it is not endorsed by most humanists and social scientists and is even less common in other disciplines. What is more common, and by no means restricted to the intelligentsia, is a more limited cognitive relativism.

1. Cf. Ernest Gellner, "Relativism and Universals," in *Rationality and Relativism*, ed. Martin Hollis and Steven Lukes (Cambridge: MIT Press, 1982), pp. 181–200.
2. Patrick Gardiner, "German Philosophy and the Rise of Relativism," *The Monist* 64 (April 1981), 138–54.

Science has enormous prestige in our culture. Its successes are many and obvious. In these circumstances people find it difficult to believe that science is not objective—that its procedures are not objectively valid, and that the truths that it progressively discovers are not reflections of objective reality. The realm of value or culture (religion, morality, art, philosophy, and so on), on the other hand, is not clearly progressive nor are its successes so striking or obvious. It is not surprising, then, that many have concluded that the rules for thinking in these realms are defective—that in these areas there are no objectively valid standards of rationality and thus no truths that are independent of the cultural systems that constitute them.

Now one of the more striking differences between science and the realm of culture and value is the (apparent) fact that there is a fair amount of agreement in the former and nothing but endless disputes and disagreements in the latter. Scientists seem able to resolve their disputes by applying their criteria and to arrive at a rough consensus. By contrast, disputes between philosophers or religious believers, or between the spokesmen of different cultures and ways of life, appear to be no nearer a resolution than in the past. Objectivity and agreement, on the one hand, and subjectivity or relativity and disagreement, on the other, thus appear to be correlated. It therefore is not surprising that attacks on the objectivity of science typically attempt to show that the apparent consensus is illusory and that defenses of the objectivity of philosophy or morality often try to show that a rough agreement of fundamental assumptions and procedures underlies the appearance of diversity.

But none of this amounts to an argument. Even if the association of agreement and objectivity and of disagreement and subjectivity or relativity is natural, why should disagreement be a *good reason* for cognitive relativism?

When Disagreement Is Relevant

1. Relativistic responses to diversity sometimes rest on one or both of two assumptions, namely, (1) that the function of modes of argument or methods of investigation is to resolve disputes concern-

ing truth or falsity, and (2) that no rationally adequate method leads to inconsistent results.

It seems patent that the methods used in religion, morality, and the humanities or social sciences fail to resolve fundamental disputes, and indeed, lead their practitioners to inconsistent conclusions. It appears to follow that these methods do not achieve their purpose and are thus rationally inadequate. It is a short step to the conclusion that they are not objectively valid.

The first assumption is ambiguous.[3] It could mean (1a) that the function of a mode of argument or method of reasoning is to determine the truth or falsity of the propositions under investigation, or it could mean (1b) that their purpose is to produce agreement with respect to the truth or falsity of the propositions in question. (1a) is clearly true, but (1b) is not. Disagreements among those employing the relevant procedures clearly indicate a functional failure, however, only if (1b) is true.

The second assumption is also ambiguous. It could mean (2a) that no method that generates inconsistent results is rationally adequate, or it could mean (2b) that no method is rationally adequate if those who use it reach conclusions that are inconsistent with one another.

A method *generates* inconsistent results if one cannot correctly apply it and avoid inconsistency. (An example would be a set of deductive rules based on a version of first-order predicate logic with inconsistent axioms.) Methods like these should be distinguished from others that are coherent but have criteria whose application requires judgment. Nothing in the nature of the latter compels those who use them to embrace inconsistencies. But good judgment does admit of degrees. Two people may therefore employ the criteria, make no egregious mistakes, and yet arrive at different and inconsistent results.

With this in mind, I suggest that (2a) is clearly true but (2b) is not. The fact that different practitioners of a mode of argument or method of investigation sometimes arrive at incompatible results is therefore inconclusive.

3. As Roger Trigg has pointed out in *Reason and Commitment* (Cambridge: Cambridge University Press, 1973), p. 126.

Note that one is unlikely to notice the distinction between (1a) and (1b), or (2a) and (2b), if one assumes that rationally adequate methods must be algorithms. Truth tables can be effectively used not only to ascertain the truth value of compound propositions but also to resolve disagreements conclusively. And because their employment does not require judgment, a pattern of inconsistent results among skilled users would suggest a deficiency in the methods themselves.

The argument we are examining in this subsection is thus defective. It is not clear why a person should think that rationally adequate methods must be algorithms. On the contrary, there are excellent reasons for thinking that they should not be. The criteria for determining whether someone really loves another, or a war is justified, or a painting is a good piece of work are complex and imprecise. This very imprecision is a virtue. For if the criteria were more precise, they would be less flexible, less useful for dealing with complex or novel situations. Whether imprecision is a structural fault depends on the nature of the subject matter. Methods need not be algorithms. If they are not, then the fact that those who more or less judiciously employ them frequently differ with respect to their application does not entail that the methods are not objective.

2. Another widely employed argument must be taken more seriously. Modern relativism is rooted in Kant as well as in Herder. Kant's contribution is the claim that knowledge and perception reflect not only the action of the world on us but also the concepts, categories, principles, and ways of thinking we bring to our experience. This claim has been widely accepted by the modern western intelligentsia, and its adoption does not commit one to subjectivism or relativism. But suppose that (pace Kant) different persons or cultures or schools of thought approach experience with different and incompatible principles and categories, and that there are no nonarbitrary ways of adjudicating between them. Both suppositions are widely believed to be true. Neither subjectivism nor relativism strictly follows (for it is logically possible that one set of competing principles and categories is, in fact, objectively true or valid). But it

does seem to follow that a *claim* that any given principle or mode of reasoning is objectively true or valid is arbitrary. It if is, then the core of subjectivism or relativism has been established.

In the previous subsection, I suggested that to the extent to which long-standing disagreements in philosophy, the social sciences, the humanities, and so on reflect the imprecision of the standards of reasoning employed in those areas, their existence provides little support for either subjectivism or relativism. But suppose that these disagreements provide evidence for thinking that different persons or cultures or schools of thought bring different and incompatible principles, categories, and modes of thinking to bear on experience, and thus construct or interpret experience in different ways. Suppose further that there are no adequate or nonarbitrary ways of adjudicating between them. In that case, subjectivist or relativist conclusions *may* be called for. For the best explanation of persistent disagreement and the absence of progress in ethics, metaphysics, religion, and so on, may be that there is no objective fact of the matter. Ethical, metaphysical, and religious beliefs, for example, have a variety of social and psychological causes; but they are *not* controlled by the beliefs' objects. (Relativism may also be implied by "There are no nonarbitrary ways of deciding between competing conceptions of rationality." If commitment to a standard of rationality is *necessarily* capricious, or *cannot* be supported by good reasons,[4] then subjectivism or relativism seem called for. But note that *circularity* is not arbitrariness. Commitment to our perceptual practices is not arbitrary even though we cannot justify our confidence in their reliability without circularity.[5] People have sometimes embraced relativism too quickly because they have confused the two.)

3. The conclusion seems to be this. Disagreement is relevant to the dispute between subjectivists or relativists and their adversaries if

---

4. Self-evidence can be a good reason.

5. A commitment to our perceptual practices is not arbitrary because they are well entrenched, consistent with our other practices and apparently successful in achieving their object (successful interaction with the physical environment). William Alston argues that something analogous is true of Christian (and e.g., Buddhist) practice.

and only if it satisfies the following conditions: First, the disagreements are over principles and modes of reasoning, not over how
these principles and modes of reasoning are to be applied in cases
falling under them. Principled differences in the application of criteria whose use requires judgment are fully compatible with objec-
tivism and nonrelativism. To suppose that they are not is mistakenly
to think that the objectivist or nonrelativist is committed to the existence of algorithms for determining (objective) truth and falsity.

Second, there are no nonarbitrary ways of resolving the disagreements.

These conditions imply a third: The disagreements over principles and modes of reasoning are fundamental; they are not due to
the imprecision of yet more basic principles and procedures to
which the parties implicitly or explicitly appeal in the course of
their dispute. (Scientific disputes between advocates of rival paradigms, or between [e.g.] cognitive psychologists and behaviorists,
may thus have less bearing on the question of relativism than is
sometimes supposed. Insofar as these disputes can be traced to different applications of such imprecise criteria as coherence, simplicity, scope, explanatory adequacy, and so forth, relativism cannot be
read off their face.)

A lack of attention to this point vitiates some arguments for relativism. For example, in attempting to show that competing theories
and standards are often incommensurable, Richard Rorty appeals
to the controversy between Galileo and Bellarmine.[6] The latter argued that although Copernican astronomy is perhaps "an ingenious
heuristic device for, say, navigational purposes," scripture shows
that Ptolemaic astronomy is roughly correct. Defenders of the new
astronomy argued that scripture is irrelevant to the points at issue.
Rorty thinks that the dispute involved fundamentally different understandings of such apparently common values as "rationality,"
"disinterestedness," "consideration of all relevant evidence," and so
on. But his example does not show this. What it shows is that judgments of relevance often depend on other judgments. For example,

6. Richard Rorty, *Philosophy and the Mirror of Nature* (Princeton: Princeton University Press, 1980), pp. 332–33.

whether Ptolemaic astronomy and Aristotelian science are embedded in scripture or are simply interpretations of it, whether Christianity and therefore its books are or are not the work of "priestcraft,"[7] and so on. Now there is no indication of substantive disagreement on what is relevant to *these* questions or on what arguments and objections would have a serious bearing on them. This example, and others like it, pose a threat to the nonrelativist only if it can be shown that disagreements over what counts as "true," "rational," or "good evidence" appear at the most basic level. For if there *is* agreement at that level, then disagreement at lower levels can, in principle, be resolved by shared standards at the higher level. The only relevant diversity, then, is a diversity of fundamental standards and there may be less disagreement at that level than is sometimes supposed. The case for such diversity is at least inconclusive.[8]

I have thus far assumed that *actual* disagreements alone count. But relativists sometimes argue that whether disagreements are actual is not important. All that matters is that they be *possible*.[9] They need not even be possible for *us*. For as Husserl points out, the bare possibility of differently constituted beings with different and incommensurable notions of truth and rationality raises the specter of relativism.[10]

This contention must be viewed with caution. For cognitive relativism to be more than a bare possibility of thought, the alternative standards must be capable of being adopted, that is, it must be possible to incorporate them into a way of life. Actual disagreement is important because it shows that this condition is met.

Consider, in this connection, Mādyamika's (and Zen's) repudiation of logic. First, it involves a conscious and deliberate rejection of a way

7. The first was a seventeenth-century debate (for the authority of scripture was generally admitted on both sides). The second was an eighteenth-century controversy.

8. See in this connection Robin Horton, "Tradition and Modernity Revisited," in *Rationality and Relativism*, pp. 201–60.

9. Cf. Barry Barnes and David Bloor, "Relativism, Rationalism, and the Sociology of Knowledge," in *Rationality and Relativism*, pp. 21–43.

10. Edmund Husserl, *Logical Investigations*, vol. 1 (New York: Humanities Press, 1970), chap. 7.

of thinking that it admits is natural or normal. Second, the enlightened continue to use ordinary canons of reasoning when doing science or engaging in everyday affairs; the canons of logic are thought to be appropriate in *those* realms (although not at the level of deep truth). Finally, Mādyamika's (although not Zen's) repudiation of logic is based on arguments that allegedly show that the canons of logic are incoherent. The importance of these facts is this. To the best of my knowledge, this strand of Buddhism provides the only clear example of a group of sane people who systematically repudiate fundamental principles of reasoning. If their arguments are defective, as I believe them to be, then the most that this example shows is that by a process of autoconditioning (various techniques of meditation) some people can at certain moments (or at a certain level) adopt alternative standards of thinking or (perhaps more accurately) no standards at all. It is not clear why this should cast any more doubt on these principles than the fact that I can systematically derange my senses[11] casts (real) doubt on the validity of sense perception.

Consider two further points: First, the fact that we can describe alternatives is not sufficient to create real difficulties. For example, I can describe a logical system whose axioms incorporate a denial of the axioms of arithmetic and first-order logic, or a mode of empirical reasoning based on counterinduction. Yet why should the non-relativist be bothered by that? That systems like these can be described would not even show that commonly accepted axioms and principles are not self-evident!

The second point is this. The claim that there either are, or could be, a variety of standards of truth and rational validity presupposes some sort of generic understanding of what counts as a (good) reason, truth claim, and so on, for without such an understanding one would have no reason to call these norms standards of truth and rational validity. The claim thus seems to presuppose precisely what extreme relativists such as Barry Barnes and David Bloor deny—the existence of more or less system-neutral notions of (good) reason, truth, validity, and so forth.[12]

11. And for certain purposes might wish to do so.
12. Cf. Barnes and Bloor, "Relativism," passim. How strong is this point? The diverse sets of standards might bear no more than a family resemblance to each

The fact that we can describe outré systems of thought and (at least in a general way) conceive of the possibility of beings whose faculties are systematically different from our own is relevant only if the nonrelativist must refute skepticism successfully.

The core of skepticism is its insistence that there is no more reason to believe that familiar ways of thinking engage the real nature of things than to suppose that quite different and incompatible ways of thinking do so. Its power lies in the impossibility of providing noncircular demonstrations of the superiority of any particular system (i.e., on the impossibility of effectively silencing Cartesian doubts). If the nonrelativist must silence Cartesian doubts, then the bare possibility of alternative systems is sufficient to raise the specter of relativism. But if (as it seems to me) it is not incumbent on her to do so, then it is not enough to show that alternatives are possible. One must also show that they could be employed by beings who are significantly similar to us, and have notions of truth, good reason, and so on that are not that different from our own. For if there are standards of this sort, then it seems incumbent on the nonrelativist to justify her belief that her own are superior to those she rejects. The only reasonably conclusive way of showing that they could be adopted, however, is by discovering human beings who actually employ them. Merely possible systems of thought *would* be relevant *if* they could be adopted. But the only way of making sure that they could would be by imaginatively placing them in the context of a whole way of life and tracing their ramifications for it. I doubt that this could be done in enough detail to warrant confidence in any conclusions we might draw from such an account.

I conclude, then, that either the case for relativism depends on a radical skepticism that insists on the silencing of Cartesian doubts (and in that case at least some of those who now find relativism appealing might wish to reconsider) or that actual disagreements alone are relevant. (The disagreements that concern us are, of course, real and therefore relevant. Views such as Edwards's or James's are hotly contested.)

---

other. Would not this be sufficient to justify applying expressions like "standards of truth" or "norms of rationality" even though there were no *common* notions of truth and rationality?

Basic Disagreements

But suppose that one grants that actual disagreements over basic standards of rationality alone need be taken seriously. There are three kinds of disagreement at this level.

For one thing, different weights are sometimes assigned to shared criteria. One may assign more weight to the demand for consistency or coherence, for example, than for explanatory adequacy (or vice versa). Modern western science and philosophy probably assign more weight to consistency and coherence than traditional societies do, although the differences should not be exaggerated. (As Robin Horton points out,[13] members of traditional societies *are* bothered by contradiction "when it is thrust under their noses," and a certain amount of incoherence [though not inconsistency] appears to be tolerated in science when this seems the price of explanatory adequacy. The use of both wave and particle models of light provides an example.) There is of course some consensus concerning the relative weights of our criteria. To the best of my knowledge everyone regards inconsistency or explanatory inadequacy as more serious than undue complexity.

There also appear to be differences in the way some shared criteria are interpreted. This is perhaps most obvious with respect to the demand for explanatory adequacy.

A good theory must "illuminate" the facts that it is designed to explain, deepen our "understanding" of the subject matter, and "satisfactorily" answer "relevant" questions. But how this is understood varies.

Lorraine Code points out that "knowing about" should be distinguished from knowing how and knowing that. For example, knowing about impressionism is not the same as knowing how to paint (even knowing how to paint an impressionist picture). Nor is it the same as knowing that a particular painting is impressionist or that Pissaro was an impressionist.[14] "Knowing about" involves understanding, and what counts as understanding is affected by historical context.

13. Horton, "Tradition," p. 242.
14. Lorraine Code, "The Importance of Historicism for a Theory of Knowledge," *International Philosophical Quarterly* 22 (June 1982), 157–74.

Michel Foucault has argued that what counts as knowledge varies from century to century. The sixteenth century believed that knowledge was largely constituted by a grasp of analogies, correspondences, and similitudes. The seventeenth and eighteenth centuries identified knowledge with the mastery of tables, lists, taxonomies, and classifications and with the analysis of "representations" or "ideas." The nineteenth century thought that genuine knowledge was provided by functional explanations, developmental theories, and historical accounts.[15] Although oversimplified, the phenomena Foucault discusses are real.

I suggest, however, that it is less accurate to describe these shifts as changes in what counts as knowledge than as changes in what counts as *significant* knowledge, or "grasp."

We can approach the problem from another angle. As Gary Gutting points out, the type of consensus found in the natural sciences differs from that found in the social sciences and humanities. During periods of normal inquiry, certain solutions are regarded as paradigmatic in the natural sciences. They are paradigmatic not only in the sense that "everyone in their fields would agree" that they are "good pieces of work" but also in the sense that there is general agreement that these solutions "should be the guide to all further work," that they "eliminate the need for foundational discussions of how inquiry in the relevant domain should be conducted." This sort of consensus does not exist in the social sciences and humanities. (Compare, for example, Newton's solutions of certain problems in mechanics with Freud's solution of certain problems in abnormal psychology or Harold Bloom's analyses of certain poetic texts.)[16] I suggest that the lack of consensus reflects differences about what counts as understanding or grasp.

Or consider the fact that paradigms differ as to which problems are regarded as important and which data are thought to require explanation. Pre-Daltonian chemistry, for example, was concerned with ex-

15. Michel Foucault, *The Order of Things: An Archaeology of the Human Sciences* (New York: Vintage, 1970).
16. See Gary Gutting, "Paradigms and Hermeneutics: A Dialogue on Kuhn, Rorty, and the Social Sciences," *American Philosophical Quarterly* 21 (January 1984), 1–15.

plaining "the observable qualities of chemical substances" and "the qualitative changes they undergo during chemical reactions." Daltonian chemistry, on the other hand, concerned itself with "weight relations and proportions in chemical reactions." Each type of chemistry was quite successful in solving its own problems but much less successful in solving those of its rival.[17] These approaches incorporated different ideas concerning which problems were important and which data most needed explanation and thus incorporated different standards of explanatory adequacy. Similar differences are reflected in metaphysical and religious disputes. For example, Christianity appears to believe that it is more important to provide an illuminating account of sin and guilt than to explain suffering (though it tries to do both). Buddhists, on the other hand, think that suffering is what primarily requires explanation (although it too offers explanations of guilt and moral failure). Certain forms of empiricism, materialism, and positivism believe that the primary data for metaphysics are provided by the sciences but idealisms are more impressed by the nature and achievements of art, morality, and religion.

If I am correct, differences with respect to what counts as knowledge or what solutions are paradigmatic, and differences with respect to the identification of problems and salient data, are differences concerning the proper *interpretation* of the demand for explanatory adequacy. Although important, they are not conflicts between different and incommensurable criteria. (Granted, there is more disagreement over what counts as understanding or grasp than over what counts as coherence or simplicity. But then the criterion is vaguer.)

But there *is* disagreement over at least one basic standard. The so-called pragmatic criterion requires that we judge metaphysical systems by whether they enable their adherents to come to terms with life successfully. The relevance of criteria like consistency and explanatory power is not in dispute among reflective people, but the pragmatic criterion is. That a worldview enables its adherents to come to terms with life may be a reason for *adopting* it but does not

17. See Gerald Doppelt, "Kuhn's Epistemological Relativism: An Interpretation and Defense," in *Relativism: Cognitive and Moral*, ed. Michael Krausz and Jack W. Meiland (Notre Dame, Ind.: University of Notre Dame Press, 1982), p. 122. The original version of this paper appeared in *Inquiry* 21 (1978).

seem to be a reason for believing it to be a better, or truer, or more adequate account of reality. Good explanations may not be life enhancing. And yet James could be right. Intelligence's theoretical and practical demands cannot be neatly separated, and one of the demands the mind makes is that the world make moral sense. If so, then (all else being equal) systems that enable us to come to terms with life may be more rationally satisfying than those that do not. Again, a plausible explanation of the fact that adoption of a worldview leads to human flourishing is that its account of things is roughly right.

The legitimacy of the criterion is nonetheless controversial. And even those who do accept it disagree about how to interpret it. For example, does it (only) require that one be able to live coherently in accordance with it?[18] Does it require systems to be effective instruments in coming to terms with the contingencies of human existence (T. S. Eliot's birth, copulation, and death)? Or must they lead to human flourishing? Note that these different interpretations lead to different assessments. Certain forms of skepticism are ruled out on the first interpretation but little else. If religiosity is a deep fact about human nature, secular humanism will be ruled out on the third interpretation but not (clearly) on the second.[19]

Finally, there are differences with respect to the epistemic virtues. The distinction between criteria such as scope, consistency, explanatory adequacy, and so on and these virtues is roughly analogous to that between the rules of a game and the skills and excellences ideally possessed by its players. I have in mind such virtues as intellectual honesty, commitment to the presentation of a reasoned case, a willingness to submit one's views to scrutiny, fairness to one's intellectual opponents, and so forth. There is some reason to think that a respect for these virtues is confined to the intellectual elites of nontraditional

18. And this in turn may or may not be interpeted as coherently living an *ordinary* human life in accordance with it.

19. Of course there are also disagreements over what counts as human flourishing as our conceptions of human flourishing depend on what we value and think human beings need. But these differences of opinion are best understood as disagreements over the *application* of the criterion rather than as disagreements over its interpretation.

cultures. The epistemic value of the virtues of the heart is at least equally controversial.

If the argument of this section is sound, there are real differences at the most fundamental level—differences over the legitimacy of at least one basic criterion, differences with respect to the weight that should be assigned to the others, differences in the interpretation of shared criteria, and differences with respect to the appropriate epistemic virtues. Do these disagreements provide evidence for relativism?

Disagreement and Objectivity

1. That the standard epistemic virtues are not prized in traditional societies provides little support for relativism.

Horton has pointed to a significant difference between modern western society and traditional African societies. As new problems and experiences arise, accepted theories and beliefs are altered to deal with them. But in traditional societies, these alterations typically consist of adjustments within, and modifications of, an inherited framework. There is little evidence of any tendency to construct or consider "a plurality of competing theoretical frameworks." What is lacking is not so much an awareness of competing frameworks as the presence of alternatives that "are being aggressively projected into" the thinker's mind "by other thinkers who wish to obliterate his own preferred theory."

Horton argues that the absence of competing frameworks also explains other differences between traditional societies and modern western society. For example, without a plurality of theories, "there is little to promote the sort of continuous critical monitoring of the theoretical framework which we associate with cognitive 'modernism.'" Although members of traditional societies are bothered by a contradiction "when it is thrust under their noses," the absence of "critical assaults of other thinkers committed to rival frameworks"[20] encourages a certain obliviousness to contradictions or incoherences

20. Together with the fact that theory is essentially "applied theory," which "tends to be developed and mobilized piece meal, as particular kinds of practical exigency arise" (Horton, "Tradition," p. 242).

that seem obvious to a critical outsider. Again, criteria such as "simplicity, scope, degree of dependence on ad hoc assumptions, predictive power," and so on, are not explicitly formulated or clearly developed, for they are essentially comparative criteria and there is "nothing to apply them to."[21]

Suppose that Horton is right and that nontraditional societies are distinguished from traditional societies by (among other things) the presence of competing theories and aggressive partisans of those theories who actively promote them. The fact that the standard epistemic virtues are not recognized in traditional societies can be easily explained. In the absence of competition there is no need for fair play and thus for the norms that define it and the virtues that internalize those norms and render them effective.

Nor is it clear why this should support relativism. That these norms are not formulated in conditions in which the need for them is not pressing and is therefore unrecognized no more shows that these norms are only relatively valid than the fact that norms of civil justice are not formulated before the emergence of civil society shows that the latter are.

But our problem cannot be disposed of so easily. For conflicting views of the epistemic virtues are not confined to differences between modern western and traditional societies. The dispute between James and William Clifford is an example.[22] The differences in temperament to which Newman calls our attention also involve (implicit) conflicts over the nature of epistemic virtue. These differences are not differences in modes or principles of reasoning. Reasoners with dissimilar temperaments appeal to the same criteria (simplicity, consistency, explanatory power, and so on) and employ the same patterns of inference (modus ponens, for example, induction, or inference to the best explanation). The inferential behavior of reasoners whose temperaments differ may nonetheless express different norms of epistemic behavior. That one should allow one's longing for revelation to affect one's assessment of the evidence for it, for instance, or that one should view claims about the supernatural with

21. Horton, "Tradition," pp. 223, 227, 241–42.
22. See James's "The Will to Believe," in *The Will to Believe and Other Essays in Popular Philosophy* (New York, c. 1896; reprint, New York: Dover, 1956).

incredulity. Or more generally, that one should sometimes allow one's heart to affect one's evaluation of the evidence, or that one should be less concerned to believe truth than to avoid error.[23] (The distinction between principles of reasoning and epistemic norms is roughly this: If one violates the former, one commits a fallacy. If one violates the latter, one fails to perform an epistemic duty or display an appropriate epistemic virtue.)

The most serious disagreements concerning the nature of rationality are over the epistemic value of the heart. In this respect, the dispute between Clifford and James is paradigmatic. What *explains* our culture's tendency to doubt the heart's epistemic value is the prestige of the physical sciences in which our subjectivity is epistemically irrelevant and perhaps even harmful. (Cultures in which religion is centrally important regard its influence as epistemically benign.) But to explain the disagreement is not to minimize it.

The problem is aggravated by the fact that differences in epistemic temperament have ramifications that extend beyond a commitment to diverse epistemic virtues. The character of one's heart or passional nature can affect one's interpretation and weighting of criteria as well as their application to particular cases. For example, those with truly benevolent hearts will find teleological or personal explanations of deep metaphysical facts illuminating, but many of those with unconverted hearts will not. If one's epistemic behavior is exclusively determined by the attitudes, dispositions, and sentiments constituting the standard intellectual virtues, one is not likely to find explanations in terms of symbolic correspondences and affinities satisfactory. Newman has shown how our temperament can affect the weight we assign evidence. And James has pointed out that minds such as Spinoza's that have a passion for simplicity will privilege very different criteria from minds that have a passion for distinguishing such as Hume's. Are we therefore faced with a residue of sheer subjectivity at the most basic level? And if we are, is relativism escapable?

2. James did not believe that the promptings of our passional nature should be uncritically accepted. Subjective or biographical fac-

---

23. In some cases these implicit norms would be repudiated if the reasoner were to become conscious of them.

tors and the basic decisions and values they affect are themselves subject to rational scrutiny.

Consider disagreements over the weighting of criteria. Assignments of weight are themselves subject to criticism that makes use of the same or related criteria. For example, it is sometimes suggested that a relevant criterion for evaluating a worldview is its "efficacy in the life process of mankind."[24] It must, according to Frederick Ferré, be "capable of 'coming to life' for individuals, becoming . . . a usable instrument for our coping with the total environment." That is, a worldview must have a "capacity for ringing true with respect to" those who use it, enabling them to "cope successfully with the challenges of life."[25] James, of course, said something similar. And this seems right.[26] But suppose that this criterion is weighted more heavily than others. One can then argue that undue deference to it is likely to lead to a tolerance for inconsistency and incoherence and that this is itself "inefficacious" for human life. Or one might argue that an overemphasis on simplicity is likely to result in systems that are explanatorily inadequate, and attempt to show that this is the case by offering examples of systems that exhibit this failing.

Or consider disputes over the proper interpretation of explanatory adequacy. Doppelt makes an important point. Aristotelian physics assumed that an adequate physical theory must explain the nature of gravitational forces. Nineteenth-century Newtonian physics did not. But it did employ its own standards of explanatory adequacy, in particular the ability of a theory to provide precise and accurate predictions of the quantitative aspects of physical phenomena. Each school of thought, employing its own standards, thus arrived at incompatible judgments concerning the comparative adequacy of the two types of physics. Their standards of explanatory adequacy are, in that sense, incommensurable. Yet as Doppelt points out, they are not incommensurable in the strong sense that no theory could satisfy

24. Paul Tillich, *Systematic Theology*, vol. 1 (Chicago: University of Chicago Press, 1951), p. 105.

25. Kent Bendell and Frederick Ferré, *Exploring the Logic of Faith* (New York: Association Press, 1962), p. 171.

26. The pressure of this demand may partly explain why only some alternative principles and standards pose a real problem to the nonrelativist.

both.[27] Nor does it follow that a theory would not be better if it did[28] or that the parties to the dispute could not be persuaded that it would. I am suggesting, in other words, that rival interpretations of explanatory adequacy are not always incompatible, for each interpretation may succeed in isolating an aspect of the demand for explanatory adequacy that ideally should be met by a comprehensive theory.

An interpretation's claim to do so can, in principle, be supported by argument. That a particular type of explanation or mode of understanding is illuminating and should therefore play a role in a comprehensive theory might be supported (for example) by arguments showing that other types or modes neglect certain aspects of the explicandum or are unable to account for certain types of phenomena, that is, by an appeal to the criterion of scope.

(Does the notion that an adequate explanatory account provides a grasp of analogies and correspondences also isolate an aspect of explanatory adequacy? Perhaps not, although it should be noted that this demand is not peculiar to the sixteenth century but again surfaces in Coleridge, Emerson, Thoreau, and others who were motivated by a desire for what Charles Taylor calls "attunement" to the cosmos.[29] Nor is it clear that a comprehensive theory would not be better if it provided the sort of illumination associated with attunement as well as accurate and precise explanations of the quantitative aspects of natural phenomena and plausible accounts of the nature of natural forces. Physical theory, as we know it, would furnish only part of a theory of this kind, but that seems irrelevant.)

Disputes over norms of epistemic behavior are not basic either if one means by this that there is nothing further to appeal to. Philosophical arguments supporting the heart's epistemic value appeal to common standards—the ability to illuminate the nature of actual inquiry, for example, or objections defused. (Newman's *Grammar* is an example of the first. Chapter 4 of this book is an instance of the second.) Attacks on the proposed standard appeal to similar criteria.

27. Doppelt, "Kuhn's Epistemological Relativism," pp. 131–32.
28. In fact, Kuhn has argued that Einsteinian physics pretty well meets the explanatory demands of both Aristotelian and nineteenth-century physics.
29. Charles Taylor, "Rationality," in *Rationality and Relativism*, pp. 87–105.

Norms of epistemic behavior can also be supported by metaphysical theories that are justified by appealing to criteria such as simplicity, explanatory power, and so forth. Edwards's theistic metaphysics is an example. Attacks on proposals such as Edwards's or James's are often partly grounded in a naturalistic metaphysics that is supported by appeals to the same standards.[30] Or again, claims that a character trait is an epistemic virtue can be defended or attacked by using the pragmatic criterion, that is, by arguing that its possession does or does not facilitate the formation of systems of belief that are "efficacious in the life process of mankind."

Arguments like these are of course circular because our cognitive temperament and epistemic habits affect what we *count* as illuminating or efficacious. (The circle involved in justifying our criteria by employing the same or related criteria is analogous.) In Chapter 4 I argued that circles of this sort need not be vicious. But the important points at present are these. (1) No criterion, weighting, or norm is immune to rational criticism and debate. Criteria, their weighting and interpretation, and the epistemic virtues can be assessed by employing the same procedures we use in *applying* our general criteria to particular theories. Both the assessment and application of general criteria call for judgment. The same sorts of consideration are appealed to in both cases, and no factor in the process is irreducibly subjective in the sense that it is beyond the scope of reason—that its claim on our assent cannot be called into question, attacked, or defended by arguments ultimately employing the same or related criteria. Furthermore, (2) Our criteria, weightings, and norms are (as a body) potentially reflexive; they can in principle meet their own standards.

3. Are our modes or inquiry objectively valid or not? At least some of our criteria may be self-certifying in the sense that they can be validated by a process of inquiry that observes them. Mill and the utilitarians appear to me to have been right in thinking (1) that there is good reason to believe that an opinion is sound only if it has withstood searching criticism, and (2) that if those who have

30. Though I cannot prove it, I suspect that suspicion of the heart's influence on reasoning is partly fueled by the metaphysical conviction that (in James's words) the universe is "alien" and not "friendly."

thought deeply about a matter agree under conditions of free and untrammeled inquiry, there is good reason to suppose that the opinions on which they agree have successfully withstood criticism.[31] To the extent to which our general criteria and norms have survived this sort of scrutiny, we have reason to think they are sound. This form of validation is circular in the sense that some of the criteria and norms whose credentials are being scrutinized will themselves be appealed to in the course of the debate over their legitimacy, weight, and proper interpretation. Yet this should not trouble us. For a similar circularity infects attempts to justify our reliance on sense perception and induction.

But notice an ambiguity. An appeal to critical consensus of this sort can take at least two forms—consensus among experts (those qualified by intelligence, training, and so on, to investigate a subject) and a consensus among rational agents, i.e., among all who are capable of engaging in rational discourse. The first is associated with John Stuart Mill, John Austin, and other classical utilitarians. The second with Jürgen Habermas (and perhaps Kant). Our test for truth or validity can therefore be understood in either of two ways depending on whether the critical debate is envisaged as taking place among experts or between rational inquirers in general.

Different interpretations yield different results. On the broader interpretation, our general criteria[32] will be self-certifying. For those standards *define* rational discourse. As Habermas has argued, any attempt to construct a rational case against these criteria (as a body) will employ them.[33] The same may be true of at least some standard epistemic virtues. For example, it seems incoherent to claim that I am *rationally* entitled to beliefs that I have achieved by ignoring ob-

31. The connection between consensus and truth provides another possible explanation of the appeal of relativism. Consensus (of a certain kind, e.g., among qualified scientists) is a criterion or sign of truth (validity), although "truth" does not *mean* consensus and consensus does not *constitute* it. The lack of consensus can therefore suggest that truth does not exist or (if it does) is not discoverable. The inference is weak, however, if the debate has not been unrestricted, has been unduly curtailed, is not guided by our general criteria, or is marred by epistemic vices.

32. With the possible (probable?) exception of the pragmatic criterion.

33. See, for example, his "Discourse Ethics: Notes on a Program of Philosophical Justification," in *The Communication Ethics Controversy*, ed. Seyla Benhabib and Fred Dallmayr (Cambridge: MIT Press, 1990), pp. 61–110.

jections and difficulties. For I can (rationally) establish my title only by *meeting* objections and *overcoming* difficulties. It is by no means clear, though, that unlimited and untrammeled discussion between rational inquirers will lead to agreement about weightings, interpretations, and the merit of such alleged epistemic virtues as true benevolence. For it is not clear that these weightings, interpretations and virtues define rational inquiry.

But if the test is *consensus among experts*, and expertise includes possession of appropriate epistemic virtues, the prospects for agreement are much better. It is not unlikely, for instance, that unlimited and untrammeled debate among those with converted hearts would eventually produce agreement over the epistemic value of true benevolence. (It does not exist at present.) Yet does not the second approach reintroduce our problem in another form? For why should expertise be interpreted in this fashion?

The difficulty is this. Our general criteria[34] are not only self-certifying in the sense that our reliance on them can be justified by appealing to them. *There are no other live options.* By contrast, suggested weightings, interpretations, and lists of epistemic virtues are essentially contested; they *have* real alternatives. Hence, although (real) doubts are out of place in the first case, they are not in the second.

Perhaps something along the lines of William Alston's response to a related difficulty[35] is the best we can manage. Epistemic virtues such as true benevolence or a tender conscience are part of an established epistemic practice that has not been shown to be unreliable and that is self-certifying in the sense that (1) it yields the intellectual and practical fruits it promises (understanding, insight, successful adaptation to reality)[36] and (2) it meets its own standards. I doubt, however, that this is sufficient in the absence of reasons for thinking that competing epistemic practices are inferior. One's position would be strongest, of course, if one could establish the superiority of one's

34. Again with the possible exception of the pragmatic criterion.
35. William Alston, *Perceiving God* (Ithaca: Cornell University Press, 1991), chap. 7.
36. These are of course internally defined; success is assessed by employing the epistemic principle whose credentials are in question. But as Alston points out, attempts to justify our reliance on sense perception and induction by appealing to their fruits encounter similar difficulties.

favored practice by successfully employing arguments addressed to anyone possessing noncontroversial epistemic virtues[37] and employing shared criteria, weightings, and interpretations. I doubt that this can be accomplished (short of the millennium). But one may be able to do something else—establish the superiority of one's epistemic practice by employing it. (It should be noted that success of this kind is not automatic. Arguably, for example, the epistemic procedure of classical utilitarianism is disutilitarian; it provides an unreliable guide to utility in practice.)

Even if this result is not fully satisfying, it should provide little comfort to the Cliffords of this world or to relativists. Not for the former, because advocates of strict and exclusive adherence to the standard epistemic virtues have the same reasons for doubt that Edwards, Newman, and James do—the existence of real alternatives that cannot be dismissed on the basis of *shared* standards and understandings. The standard position is as exposed to charges of special pleading as those it objects to.

The relativists' triumph is equally hollow. Disagreements over the epistemic value of virtues such as true benevolence are evidence for relativism only if the facts would be different if relativism were false. But given that (for example) Edwards's (nonrelativistic) version of Christian theism is true, the facts would not be different. It is hardly surprising that those who lack the appropriate epistemic virtues fail to esteem them. Hearts whose loves are constricted are not likely to appreciate the epistemic value of true benevolence.

Views such as Edwards's, Newman's, and James's can even help defuse relativism. If there *are* ethical, metaphysical, and religious facts and we have the ability to discern them, lack of progress and the persistence of deep disagreement are, on the face of it, surprising. When faced with disagreement it is therefore tempting to conclude that either there are no ethical, metaphysical, or religious facts or that our epistemic faculties are not reliable guides to their discovery. Suppose, however, that true benevolence is needed to reason rightly about "divine things" or that certain subject matters require appropriate

37. An openness to alternatives and objections, for example, but not neutrality.

dispositions, interests, or sentiments. In that case, deep disagreements are likely even if the relevant truths are objective and our epistemic faculties are reliable when functioning as they should. For some will possess the appropriate dispositions and others will not. Indeed, in the *absence* of an appeal to the epistemic importance of passional factors, it may be difficult to reconcile serious disagreement and the absence of progress with the objectivity of truth and confidence in our epistemic faculties. Not only does the approach defended in this book not *support* relativism; it may be the only means of avoiding it.

Epilogue

Suppose that views like Edwards's, Newman's, and James's *can* be defended against charges of subjectivism, circularity, and relativism. Why should we take them seriously?

One reason is this. Theists who think there are rational arguments for the truths of religion and who, in the light of their beliefs, think through the implications of their disagreements with intelligent, well-informed, honest, and philosophically astute critics will be forced to draw similar conclusions. They believe that their critics' assessment of the overall force of the evidence is in error. This error cannot plausibly be attributed to such things as lack of intelligence, unfamiliarity with relevant evidence, obvious prejudice, or an unwillingness to consider counterclaims. Edwards would ascribe it to a failure of the heart. Modern theists may be reluctant to do so—partly because of their respect for their critics and partly because of their fear of intellectual phariseeism. Yet if theism *is* true, and there *is* good evidence for it, what other explanation could there be of the failure of so many to appreciate its force? Intellectual phariseeism *is* a danger, but I suggest that its corrective is to focus on the ways in which one's own sinful proclivities infect and distort one's thinking about God.[1]

---

1. On this point, see Merold Westphal's excellent "Taking St. Paul Seriously: Sin as an Epistemological Category," in *Christian Philosophy*, ed. Thomas P. Flint (Notre Dame, Ind.: University of Notre Dame Press, 1988), pp. 200–226.

Nontheists should also take positions of this kind seriously. In the second section of Chapter 4, I argued that anyone who is convinced he is right on a matter about which there is basic dispute may be forced to adopt similar claims to account for the fact that many intelligent critics disagree with him. Of course he might refuse to offer any explanation. But without one his continued adherence to his own opinion ought to appear arbitrary both to himself and others.

That certain affections are needed to perceive the truth of religious claims is not as outré or as ad hoc as one might think. As I suggested in Chapter 4, affectivity and our cognition of value may be closely related. This is obvious if emotivism or R. M. Hare's prescriptivism are true. On these views, "perceiving" the value of something is the same thing as adopting certain attitudes toward it. But the connection is also close on various cognitive theories. In his seventh letter, for example, Plato asserts that "it is barely possible for knowledge to be engendered of an object naturally good, in a man naturally good; but if his nature is defective, as is that of most men, for the acquisition of knowledge and the so-called virtues, and if the qualities he has have been corrupted, then not even Lynceus could make such a man see. In short, neither quickness of learning nor a good memory can make a man see when his nature is not akin to the object, for this knowledge never takes root in an alien nature; so that no man who is not naturally inclined and akin to justice and all other forms of excellence, even though he may be quick at learning and remembering this and that and other things . . . will ever attain the truth that is attainable about virtue."[2]

Aristotle thought that the "major premises" of practical syllogisms "are universal judgments as to what is good for men in general, or as a rule," or what is generally good for certain classes of people, or people in certain kinds of circumstances. These principles are (partial) articulations of the good life. Only a person "in a healthy emotional state" can grasp the truth of correct principles. If his desires, impulses, and feelings have "been perverted by wrong training," he will not be able to do so. Children who have developed bad moral

2. *Plato's Epistles*, trans., with critical essays and notes, by Glenn R. Morrow (Indianapolis: Bobbs-Merrill, 1962), pp. 240–41. Lynceus was an Argonaut noted for keenness of sight.

dispositions, who have "a perverted sense of what is worth having in life," will formulate false principles of conduct. (They will, as Plato says, have a lie in their soul.)[3]

It may seem odd to place Kant in the same company, but respect for the moral law (and for persons in so far as they embody it) is arguably a cognitive emotion. More accurately, it is not a feeling *distinct* from our recognition that something is our duty which is *caused* by it; it is the "emotional side" of that recognition. In other words, respect is the form that recognition takes in a being with inclinations—it is an *aspect* of recognition, namely, its emotional resonance.[4] If this is right, then (in a being with inclinations), a certain affective state is a necessary condition of the perception of moral value.

Now on a classical view, God *is* goodness itself, that is, He *is* the supreme value, and not merely a perfect instance of it. If so, it is not surprising that properly ordered affections are needed to grasp truths about Him. Even if God cannot be *identified* with goodness, the point may still hold. As Jonathan Edwards points out, theological claims *entail* value claims. The story of creation or redemption, for example, (logically) includes value judgments. To grasp the former, we must therefore grasp the latter. Thus the doctrine of redemption cannot be understood without an adequate appreciation of sin's magnitude and horror. If Edwards is right, true benevolence is needed to appreciate them.

Metaphysical judgments may be more closely connected to our evaluations than is usually recognized. James points out that "as a rule we disbelieve all facts and theories for which we have no use. Clifford's cosmic emotions find no use for Christian feelings. Huxley belabors the bishops because there is no use for sacerdotalism in his scheme of life." When we find a use for these facts and theories, however, evidence that had not impressed us previously may now seem "good enough."[5] What we have use for, of course, depends on our needs and interests, hopes and fears.

3. H. H. Joachim, *Aristotle, The Nicomachean Ethics, A Commentary*, ed. D. A. Rees (Oxford: Clarendon, 1951), p. 211.

4. H. J. Paton, *The Categorical Imperative* (New York: Harper Torch Books, 1967), pp. 66–68. The interpretation is confirmed by what Kant says in the *Critique of Pure Judgement*, Division I, Book I, #12.

5. William James, "The Will to Believe," in *The Will to Believe and Other Essays in Popular Philosophy* (New York, 1890; reprint, New York: Dover, 1956), p. 10.

Plato also thinks that judgments of reality are affected by feelings and evaluations. In the *Phaedo* he argues that "no man's soul can feel intense pleasure and pain in anything without also at the same time believing that the chief object of these his emotions is transparently clear and utterly real."[6] (See also James who asserts that "among all sensations, the *most* belief-compelling are those productive of pleasure or of pain.")[7] If this is true, then what pains and pleases us will affect our judgments of what is and is not real. Bodily pleasures and pains, for example, drive "a rivet into the soul, pinning it down to the body and so assimilating it thereto that it believes everything to be real which the body declares so to be."[8] A person who is absorbed by bodily pleasure and pain is hence likely to be a materialist. If this line of thought is correct, and our judgments of reality are affected by our pains and pleasures, desires and fears, then rightly ordered affections may be needed to perceive things as they are.

But, clearly, passion's effect on reasoning is not always benign. Self-interest, partisanship, love or hatred can cloud our judgment. What is needed is a "critique of passional reason"—an account of the conditions under which passion does and does not enhance reasoning. How might such a theory be constructed?

One could proceed inductively. For example, psychological studies of the ways in which emotion distorts reasoning or the literature on self-deception provide samples from which we might extrapolate rules telling us when or how passion *should not* affect reasoning.

I am not sure how promising this approach is. It is easy to find cases in which emotion or passion adversely affect reasoning. Hatred, for example, may lead us to exaggerate the force of the evidence for our enemy's guilt. But one must be wary of overhasty generalization. Hatred can also make us clear-sighted. Because of it, we may notice weaknesses in the case for our enemy's claim to innocence that would be overlooked by both his friends and those who view the evidence in Bishop Butler's "cool hour." Although in individual cases

---

6. *Plato's Phaedo*, trans., with introduction and commentary by R. Hackforth (Indianapolis: Bobbs-Merrill, 1955), p. 93 (*Phaedo* 83 C).

7. William James, *Principles of Psychology*, vol. 2 (New York: Dover, 1950), p. 306.

8. *Plato's Phaedo*, p. 93 (83D).

it can be quite clear that subjectivity is or is not impairing reasoning, it may prove difficult to extrapolate useful rules.

The alternative is to take the Kantian analogy suggested by the book's subtitle seriously. Just as (on Kant's view) we cannot determine the nature or structure of pure theoretical or practical reason without provisionally determining what scientific or moral claims are true, so perhaps we cannot determine what affections are and are not epistemically beneficial without provisionally determining what metaphysical claims are correct.

Kant presupposes that scientific and moral reasoning is in order and that Newtonian science and conventional morality are fundamentally sound and then asks, "What must be the case if our reasoning is in order and the beliefs established by it are true?" Our task may be similar. As Newman and James have shown, temperament, passion, intuition, and sentiment affect the beliefs we take as basic and our attitude toward evidence. That their influence is inescapable seems equally clear. Evidentialist approaches cannot avoid it because our subjectivity affects the way in which we assess the force of arguments, the adequacy of explanations, and the plausibility of controversial assumptions. What is true of reasoning in general is true of reasoning to theological conclusions; it is shot through with "subjectivity." The best approach, then, may be to assume that some instances of this inherently "passionate" religious reasoning are sound and that some of its conclusions are correct (that God is revealed in scripture, for example, or that apparent design is evidence for His existence) and to ask "What must be true of the world and our relation to it if our religious knowledge is genuine?" and (having determined that) "Given that the world and our relation to it is like that, under what conditions is passional reasoning legitimate?"

This book has made some attempt to answer the first question.[9] How might one answer the second? One possibility is this. Some (all?) theological claims entail value claims. The nature of the latter may determine the nature of the affections needed to grasp the former. For example, Edwards thinks that the doctrine of hell is true.

---

9. Or more accurately, it has sketched the answers of Edwards, Newman, and James.

But the doctrine of hell entails that infinite punishment is deserved, and this in turn entails that sin is infinitely heinous. Edwards quite reasonably concludes that an appreciation of sin's horror is therefore needed to appreciate the doctrine's truth. Ultimately, the nature of God and our relation to Him implies that what we need is true benevolence. (In *Religious Affections* Edwards shows that true benevolence includes all other holy dispositions and thus, by implication, all other affections needed for our faculties to function effectively in reasoning to theological conclusions.)

This may be too strong. Even if true benevolence is a *sufficient* condition of reasoning soundly about divine matters,[10] it may not be necessary. To see this, consider a suggestion of C. Stephen Evans: That the subjective condition (passion, emotion, attitude) one needs to see the force of the theistic proofs is *faith*.[11] I submit that it is something less than that although faith may include it. For example, religious *hope* or *longing* may be sufficient—a kind of readiness to believe which is not yet belief itself. (Note that readiness to believe is not the same as sympathy with belief for one can have the latter without the former. Santayana or George Eliot may be examples. But one can also have the former without the latter. Although Tarwater in Flannery O'Connor's *The Violent Bear It Away* has little sympathy with his grandfather's stern faith, he finds it difficult to resist, and in the end he submits to it.) If faith is not necessary, however, then (as true benevolence includes it)[12] neither is true benevolence. Of course, one *might* think of this readiness to believe as a kind of implicit faith. But doing so obscures the distinction between belief and its potentiality. It might be better to identify it with an inchoate love of the good.[13]

10. All else (intelligence, information, training, etc.) being equal.

11. C. Stephen Evans, *Passionate Reason, Making Sense of Kierkegaard's Philosophical Fragments* (Bloomington: Indiana University Press, 1992), pp. 69–71.

12. True benevolence principally consists in the love of God and the love of God logically presupposes belief in God.

13. Of course if God is the good, an inchoate love of the good is an inchoate love of God; and because (according to Edwards) God is "in effect" being in general, it is thus also an inchoate love of being in general. But until belief becomes actual, this inchoate love of being in general is not (yet) true benevolence. For the latter includes an *active acknowledgment* of God's reality and not merely a longing for it. Note that there is some similarity between the view I am (tentatively) taking

To settle these matters, though, is beyond the scope of this book. Its purpose has been to convince the reader that (under the right conditions) passion, sentiment, and affection may be necessary conditions of using our cognitive faculties correctly. If this is true, then ethics and "logic" overlap. An ethics of belief will be an essential part of any viable concept of good reasoning. But an adequate ethics of belief must include a critique of our passional nature, a concept of normal human functioning, and so on. As a result it will be intrinsically connected with ethics as such (and ultimately with metaphysics). Plato will turn out to have been right. Good reasoning is an expression of a properly constituted human psyche.

---

here and the views of Aquinas as described by Eleonore Stump ("Aquinas on Faith and Goodness," in *Being and Goodness*, ed. Scott MacDonald [Ithaca: Cornell University Press, 1991]). But, unlike Aquinas, Edwards does not identify being and goodness. The good is being *plus* holiness, that is, being plus the love of being. Love of the good and the love of being in general are, however, logically coextensive. For anyone who loves being loves the love of being (see *True Virtue*) and hence loves the good. Similarly anyone who loves the good loves being in general as the latter is included in it.

Index

Cornell Studies in the Philosophy of Religion
EDITED BY WILLIAM P. ALSTON